The

WHEEL

of the

YEAR

The
WHEEL
of the
YEAR

*A Guide to Sabbats, Lunar Cycles,
and the Stars Above*

NIKKI VAN DE CAR

illustrated by
MALIN GYLLENSVAAN

RUNNING PRESS
PHILADELPHIA

Running Press
Hachette Book Group
1290 Avenue of the Americas, New York, NY 10104
www.runningpress.com
@Running_Press

First Edition: August 2024

Published by Running Press, an imprint of Hachette Book Group, Inc.
The Running Press name and logo are trademarks of Hachette Book Group, Inc.

The Hachette Speakers Bureau provides a wide range of authors for speaking events. To find out more, go to www.hachettespeakersbureau.com or email HachetteSpeakers@hbgusa.com.

Running Press books may be purchased in bulk for business, educational, or promotional use. For more information, please contact your local bookseller or the Hachette Book Group Special Markets Department at Special.Markets@hbgusa.com.

The publisher is not responsible for websites (or their content) that are not owned by the publisher.

Print book cover and interior design by Susan Van Horn

Library of Congress Cataloging-in-Publication Data has been applied for.

ISBNs: 978-0-7624-8748-6 (hardcover), 978-0-7624-8750-9 (ebook)

Printed in China

1010

10 9 8 7 6 5 4 3 2 1

Contents

Introduction . . . vii

Author's Note . . . ix

SAMHAIN *. . . 1*

YULE *. . . 17*

IMBOLC *. . . 35*

OSTARA *. . . 49*

BELTANE *. . . 67*

LITHA *. . . 81*

LAMMAS *. . . 97*

MABON *. . . 109*

Conclusion . . . 127

Acknowledgments . . . 129

Index . . . 130

Introduction

LIVE A LIFE FILLED
WITH MAGIC

I T'S A WORTHY GOAL TO SEEK OUT A LIFE BRIMMING WITH enchantment to be sure, but it's not exactly easy to achieve. How do we find the magic in working through a grocery list, slogging through emails and texts, or doing laundry and errands—all those hassles of everyday life? A life filled with magic can feel unreachable.

And yet magic is always with us. The truth is that magic is present in every moment, no matter how ordinary or mundane it may seem. Magic thrives in the everyday ... it's just a matter of reminding yourself it is there.

The Wheel of the Year: A Guide to Sabbats, Lunar Cycles, and the Stars Above is a handbook that will guide you in finding magic throughout a full year of your life. It will help you not only understand, but also fully embody, the practice of living a magical life. Drawing from ancient traditions and modern insights, this almanac invites you to embrace the cycles of nature and the celestial dance of the stars. While the Gregorian calendar does not really match the music of the spheres—and neither do our schedules—we can do our best to align our lives with the rhythms of the natural world. The beginning of each month includes an overall theme of that lunar cycle derived from various cultures and Indigenous traditions of North America. And every week, you'll be offered guidance on what to put your attention on and given a suggested spell. Each spell is crafted to harmonize with the astrological energies of the week, deepening your magical practice.

The weekly prompts are punctuated by a deeper look into the pagan sabbats, or holidays, of Samhain, Yule, Imbolc, Ostara, Beltane, Litha, Lammas, and Mabon, each marking a significant spoke on the ever-turning wheel of the year. Since the traditions of the wheel of the year come from Western Europe, the majority of the practices and folklore covered in this book will derive from those traditions—and look at the wheel of the year from the perspective of the Northern Hemisphere—though there will be references to other cultural celebrations scattered here and there. Each sabbat represents a moment of transformation and reflection, allowing us to attune ourselves to the natural world, honor the changing seasons, and align ourselves with the magic that surrounds us. By embracing these ancient celebrations, we tap into the collective wisdom of our ancestors.

The rituals, meditations, spells, and insights gathered here are designed to empower you, awaken your intuition, and encourage a deeper connection to the natural world and the magic that goes along with it. You are the orchestrator of your own journey. As you immerse yourself in the wisdom of the sabbats and embrace the celestial energies, let this book be a companion, illuminating your path, inspiring your creativity, and sparking your magic . . . every day.

Author's Note

You might notice that this almanac lists only forty-eight weeks, while there are technically fifty-two weeks in a year. Where have those missing four weeks gone?

The truth is that those four weeks—and the concept of a "week" in the first place—belong to the Gregorian calendar, and not to the cycles of the moon and the heavens. A lunar cycle is technically 29.5 days long, which certainly doesn't align with our calendar in any way. You'll also note that the astrological events don't *precisely* align with their assigned weeks, as, once again, the stars and our structured lives do not always match up.

So how do you work with that?

This almanac is not a *planner*. It's not going to help you stick to your schedule, manage your routine, or remember all your appointments. In fact, it is intended to help you put all of that aside. Obviously, we all live in the world and have our responsibilities, so we can't ignore our calendars entirely—but this book is an opportunity to set aside some time to live outside the bounds of our structured lives, experiencing life according to the natural cycles of the cosmos, rather than the regimented organization of Western society. It's a book that isn't bound by any calendar year, but one that you can come back to year after year, adjusting your approach and uncovering more intuitive knowledge as you go. Look at this almanac as a way to break out of your routine and find a more rhythmic, nature-based approach to daily life.

SAMHAIN

October 31

S AMHAIN MARKS THE FIRST DAY OF THE PAGAN NEW YEAR, and it begins the Season of the Witch. It is known by a variety of names in cultures the world over, including Día de Muertos, All Souls' Day, and, of course, Halloween. In Celtic pagan cultures, it marked the night after the final harvest, and any cattle left roaming the hill-sides at this point were brought down to be counted and secured for the coming cold. People would make offerings of food and drink to any spir-its who might have been walking, and they would dress in white or as a different gender to confuse and conceal themselves from any harmful forces abroad on the land.

Before the sun went down on Samhain, fields were cleared and the dried remnants were used to light bonfires. Each member of a household would place a stone near the fire, and in the morning, they would exam-ine the markings left by the ash and smoke to find out what the new year would hold for them. But more than anything, those bonfires were set to protect people from the flight of the Cailleach.

One of the original hag-witch figures of lore, the Cailleach, also known as Beira, the queen of winter, wakes from her summer sleep on Samhain and sets forth to travel with the storms, rapping her staff on the ground with the sound of thunder and freezing the earth. But as with all crone witches—like Baba Yaga, Hecate, the Fates, the Norns, and the Weird Sisters—the Cailleach can be benevolent if she so chooses, offering her protection to the wild creatures that dwell outside of our sheltering fires.

She is the Cailleach Samhain, the wise woman of the hills. She is a guardian of the old ways, and a keeper of secrets. The Cailleach is a force to be honored, and perhaps she might even grant her benevolence to us, offering her shelter to those who feel the wilderness inside.

THE NIGHT OF THE WALKING DEAD

As with any celebration that marks a new beginning, Samhain takes place in a liminal space, a hovering moment of time when all things are possible. And on Samhain, those possibilities include the walking dead.

But what does that mean, exactly? Deeply rooted in all of us is the same fear: that the dead will rise. Zombie stories have been told in one form or another for thousands of years, from ancient Greece through the Middle Ages, and they remain ever present in popular culture. The question is *why*? Why do we fear the return of our loved ones?

The reason, of course, is that they are not *meant* to return. The dead, however much we may mourn and miss them, are meant to stay as they are: buried in the earth, returned to the elements. We know perfectly well that death means the completion of a cycle and what the next turn of the wheel will be is an eternal mystery. And in truth, we do not *actually*, in our logical and waking minds, believe that the dead will rise, stumbling and rotting and perhaps trying to bite us, as they bring us into their ranks. We know better than that.

But on the night of Samhain, the world is held in a state between waking and dreaming—that liminal space, again—where all that we know to be true, as well as all that we know to be impossible, becomes a little less certain. And so we feel a twinge of irrational fear, of excitement and adrenaline, and we seek out haunted houses and scary movies, leaning in to those emotions. There is even a kind of joy in them, a pleasurable sense of dread and anticipation.

That experience is the truth of Samhain. No, the dead will not walk in the literal sense . . . but they will *feel* as if they do. They are closer to us, somehow, and that closeness can take a variety of forms.

Reaper

Depending on what we believe, death is not necessarily something to be feared. Perhaps there is an afterlife, a next life, or a continuing of consciousness that takes some other, currently unimaginable form. Whatever your faith, it is a fact that energy never dissipates; it simply reforms. And so whatever it is that animates us—the soul, if you will—can never truly vanish, either.

But for all that, we don't *know* what the next cycle will mean for us, and so we tend to live as though this is the only existence we will ever have—and it is right that we should do so! Waiting, treading water in the vast sea of life rather than swimming in it—now *that* is something we should fear. But, of course, the flip side of living as if this is all we will ever have is the constant dread of the day it stops.

We will all die. Everyone we love will die. In some sense, we are all the walking dead. This is a fear that will come to pass, and as such it is something we spend a great deal of time and energy avoiding thinking about it—for if we dwell on it for too long we can lose ourselves in it.

Samhain allows us to face this fear without drowning in it. It allows us to *play* with it: to find whimsy, laughter, and joy in death. We can walk beside it, even dance with it, and in doing so, we can feel all the more alive.

Buried Fears

Our fears are not always rational. Spiders, for instance, do good work for us, keeping house and protecting us from insects. Barring the few poisonous species, their bites are neither particularly painful nor harmful—and yet a spider can send an otherwise reasonable and courageous person screeching. We all have fears like this that are rooted in our childhoods, our family history, and perhaps even our genetics.

And we typically tend to run from spiders like we would from fast-moving zombies. Samhain provides an opportunity to sit down with those fears—a chance, once again, to play. We can dress up as a snake-monster or, conversely, as a snake-slayer. We can voluntarily enter a space we know will be filled with jump scares and murderous clowns, knowing that the thrills provided by a haunted house are all in good fun.

Regrets

Sometimes, however, our own personal walking dead are not quite so much fun to spend time with. When the veil between the past and the present is thin, our regrets tend to rise. Then what marches before us are the things we cannot change, the choices we made that we cannot unmake. We all have regrets—actions we look back on with sorrow, embarrassment, or remorse. We all make mistakes, after all.

Samhain is an opportunity to examine those mistakes and consider whether we really need to continue to carry them with us. Perhaps we can ask forgiveness for the harm we have caused? Or perhaps our regrets are for something we needn't really regret at all—our teenaged humiliations are long past, and the choices we made brought us to where we are now. For better or worse, they made us who we are, and they can inform who we choose to be.

The dead are meant to stay dead, and dwelling on our regrets usually serves no purpose. When your regrets walk the night, wave at them, acknowledge them for the ghosts they are, perhaps even thank them for the lessons they taught you—and then lay them to rest once more.

Ancestors

Perhaps the most welcome walking dead are our ancestors. They are close at hand on Samhain, so much so that in ancient times folks would bury apples at the crossroads to feed and guide the wandering dead back home. They would light lanterns and place them in the windows, and they would even set them a place at the dinner table. Thought to have originated in Scotland in the seventeenth century, this "dumb supper" would be held in silence, perhaps to allow the quiet voices of the dead to be heard. It may also have been a way to appease the spirits, and now acts as a way to connect with those who have passed.

On Día de Muertos, celebrations begin with a visit to the graves of loved ones and the creation of ancestral altars known as ofrendas, which are decorated with calendula (marigolds), candles, and papel picado, a type of beautifully cut paper. The night is spent telling stories of the deceased, laughing and celebrating them in turn, and often holding a party or a parade, complete with costumes and masks.

Most of the time, when we think of our loved ones who are no longer with us, we feel grief . . . but Samhain is a time when, once again, we can transmute our more difficult feelings into a celebration. Rather than pushing away that heaviness and dread like we usually do, Samhain is a time when we gather it in, reaping it like the final harvest of the year and then finding joy and laughter in the darkness.

SAMHAIN RITUAL TO CONNECT WITH YOUR WALKING DEAD

Before the sun sets, herd your metaphorical cattle down from the hills and reap the last of your harvest. Begin by brewing yourself a cup of tea to help you step over your internal threshold of the doorway you normally keep closed, barricading all of your walking dead. Bring a pot of water to boil, and allow one teaspoon's worth of the following mixture to steep, covered, for ten minutes:

* **Dried calendula, to connect with the dead**

* **Dried marjoram, for grief**

* **Dried mint, for clarity**

* **Dried mugwort, for divination**

* **Dried parsley, for protection**

* **Dried sage, for wisdom**

When your tea is ready, pull out your journal. Write down any thoughts that come to you, without thinking too hard about any of them. Let your mind be open, and move through the Reaper, the Buried Fears, the Regrets, and the Ancestors in turn. When your mind has emptied, go back and read what you've written. Circle or underline what you choose to explore this Samhain, and cross out or tear away all the rest. You don't need to spend any more time with those thoughts. Samhain is a time when you get to choose whether or not you will engage with what haunts you.

If you decide to connect with your ancestors on this night, you might consider building an ancestral altar, incorporating some or all of the following:

* **Images of deceased loved ones**

* **Items that belonged to them or that remind you of them**

* **Flowers, particularly marigolds, but also chrysanthemums, lilies, irises, and poppies, which all have a connection to the dead**

* **Offerings, including food and drink**

It should be noted that ancestral altars do not have to be specific to any person or persons in particular. They certainly can be, and creating a space that is dedicated particularly to, for instance, a grandparent or other loved one, can do so much to enhance your experience of their presence on Samhain. But ancestral altars can also help you connect to an unknown ancestor, someone from long, long ago, whose experiences were so different from yours today and yet whose life shaped yours in ways you cannot even perceive. It can be helpful to envision a wise woman or hermit, or perhaps a shield-maiden or knight of old, whose guidance can inspire you in the coming year. To aid in this vision, anoint yourself at your wrists, the base of your throat, and your third eye with a mixture of sage, lavender, and frankincense essential oils.

You may also want to hold a lapis lazuli, opal, malachite, or amethyst in the open palm of your nondominant hand.

Speak with whomever you are calling forth. This can be aloud, but it can also happen in your mind and heart. Listen to this ancestor, as you sit before your altar, remembering them and feeling their presence. You can envision your ancestors as a series of reflections in a mirror maze, as if they are all standing behind you—shifting likenesses of you, going back through time, but there with you now, holding all of their wisdom and experience and passing it down to you.

As the sun sets, light your bonfire. If you have a safe space where you can build an actual bonfire, that's great, but if not, simply lighting a candle is all that is required. To invoke the Cailleach, collect one or more of the following herbs that are sacred to her. If it's safe to do so (sparks may flare), sprinkle them onto the flame, though you can also simply sprinkle them around the candle.

* **Broom, which protects against harmful spirits and energies**

* **Heather, for healing**

* **Rowan, for protection and to lower the veil between worlds**

* **Willow, for healing and to lower the veil**

As you cast the herbs, ask the Cailleach for her blessing, either aloud or in your mind:

> *Cailleach, Cailleach, hear my call.*
> *I summon you from the winter's cold.*
> *Wise one, share your wisdom with me.*

Week One

THE LIGHT OF THE NOVEMBER MOON

The Frost Moon of November is also known as the Beaver Moon. Beavers symbolize hard work, determination, and cooperation, but this moon occurs as they make ready to retreat to their lodges, huddling together for warmth and protection during the long winter's rest. This week is a good time to follow their example and hunker down, settling yourself in for the coming cold and wrapping yourself in comfort.

Suggested Spell

If you have a favorite blanket, pull it out now. Maybe it's the warmest one you have, or maybe it's a little tattered, having been passed down through generations. Wrap it around your shoulders like a cloak, sealing in your warmth, and then step outside. You can do this day or night, whichever is most convenient for you. Stand just outside your door, and listen to the world. Pay attention to what you hear, whether it's car horns or birdsong or children walking home from school. Look at the leaves on the trees. Which leaves remain, and which have already turned color and fallen? There's a certain slant of light that occurs in the Northern Hemisphere at this time of year—a sharper angle, and with it a brighter, harsher brilliance. What can you see in this clear, stark daylight or under the softer beams of the moon? Stare close to the sun or at a bright object for just a moment, and then close your eyes and look at the lingering image against your eyelids, still there even though you have looked away. Keep in mind all the things that remain even when we don't necessarily pay attention to or acknowledge them—our hard work and our determination, as well as the people in our lives who help and support us.

When you've taken it all in, go back inside. Close your door firmly, shutting it all out again. Retreat to your lodge, and allow yourself the gift of doing anything that brings you comfort, whether that's rereading a beloved book, watching a favorite show, or enjoying a sweet, warm beverage.

Week Two

NEW MOON IN SCORPIO

The new moon is a sliver of possibility, and when it aligns with the constellation of Scorpio, it provides an opportunity for healing and transformation. As a deeply mysterious water sign, Scorpio is associated with emotions, and the light of this new moon can show you any emotions you've kept hidden from yourself so that you can either allow them to flow through you and inspire you or to be released into the November winds.

Suggested Spell

Sit in the dim light of the new moon, using only a small lamp or perhaps a candle. You may want to surround yourself with crystals that align with Scorpio, like obsidian, bloodstone, onyx, ruby, and tourmaline, and you may also wish to diffuse one or more of the following essential oils to further invite Scorpio's guidance:

* **Black pepper, for luck and protection**

* **Cypress, for forward-thinking and divination**

* **Juniper, for protection and creativity**

* **Myrrh, for love and creativity**

* **Patchouli, for enhancing the senses**

* **Vetiver, for grounding**

Allow yourself to listen deeply to your own intuition, specifically to your emotional guidance. What do you feel? What do your emotions have to tell you? Write down in a journal whatever comes up for you, giving yourself the freedom to let it all flow out without judgment. When you feel complete and emptied, read back over what you've written. What do you want to keep? What feels useful to you; what emotions are guiding you in a positive direction? Alternatively, what are you ready to let go of?

Week Three

SUN IN SAGITTARIUS

When the sun is in Sagittarius, we all have the opportunity for growth, expansion, and learning. As a fire sign, Sagittarius has a naturally curious and creative energy, inviting new experiences and the fresh knowledge that comes with them. This is a good time to make new friends and embrace your impulsivity. See what new adventures life has to offer you, and step over the edge of your self-imposed limitations.

Suggested Spell

Harness the optimism and inquisitiveness of Sagittarius by setting some intentions—and then acting on them right away! That person you see on your daily commute, the one who seems like someone you would get along with? This is the time to say hello and see where the conversation takes you.

If that isn't easy for you, you're not alone. Create a talisman to take with you, one that can fill you with the energy of Sagittarius when you most need it. The color of Sagittarius is purple, so find a four-by-four-inch square of purple cloth. Then add one or two of the following crystals:

* **Amber, for fiery energy**

* **Amethyst, for intuition**

* **Citrine, for creativity**

* **Tigereye, for personal power**

* **Turquoise, for communication**

Sprinkle the crystals with the following:

* **Basil, for strength and goodwill**

* **Chamomile, for calm**

* **Cinnamon, for healing and protection**

* **Ginger, for energy**

Fold up the corners of your square and tie them with a piece of string or yarn. Carry your spell bag with you as you follow Sagittarius's guidance—you can keep it in your pocket or your bag or sleep with it beneath your pillow. It will remind you that your curiosity and creativity are always available whenever you need them.

Week Four

FULL MOON IN TAURUS

Full moons are always a time for manifestation, as that is when the moon is at its brightest and showing us our possibilities with the most clarity and luminance. But in this case, the full moon is balanced by the grounding and practicality of Taurus. As a fixed earth sign, Taurus is both sensible and stubborn, and when the full moon is in Taurus, our emotions become very present—even physically so. You may feel your heart race and your eyes water when strong feelings arise. Your senses will be more attuned to the world around you.

Suggested Spell

On the day of the full moon, make it a point to get out in nature, and if it's possible to do so at night, that's even better. In all likelihood, it'll be cold out—so bundle up—but take the time to let yourself feel the natural world around you. If you've got your hands buried in your pockets, take them out. Feel the bark of the trees, hear the crunch of the leaves beneath your feet, and smell the dry November air. As you walk, consider what you want to manifest in the light of this full moon, but keep it practical. Choose one dried leaf, stone, or broken twig to bring home with you, and place it on your altar as a symbol of the pragmatic energy you are inviting into your life.

YULE

December 21

YULE OCCURS ON THE WINTER SOLSTICE, AT THE MOMENT in time when the earth is farthest from the sun, its axis tilted so sharply that the darkness reigns longer in the Northern Hemisphere than on any other night. It marks the beginning of winter, the long dark cold that sends nature to sleep, as the squirrels and frogs, bats and bumblebees lock themselves away, burrowing into what warmth they can find.

Winter can seem dead and stark; the trees are barren, all of their colors abandoned for shades of gray. The sounds of the forest are muted, at times muffled by snow. The birds have left for warmer climes, and the silence echoes in place of their songs.

And yet, there are *always* signs of life. Crows, who do not migrate for the winter, fly blackly overhead, their raucous cries a reminder that life is a celebration, even in darkness. And of course, there are those trees that refuse to sleep through the winter, but remain evergreen and bright, their vitality all the more brilliant against the winter palette of gray and white. We can turn to them for inspiration when the world feels cold and let their spirits guide us.

THE HOLLY KING

The wheel of the year is spun by the force of a battle waged between the Oak King and his brother the Holly King. They are oppositional forces, but they are also each other's mirror—where the Oak King offers growth and renewal, the Holly King offers shelter and protection, as well as the time to rest and dream of new beginnings, to prepare for the work that will be required of us in the coming spring. He also represents the wild unpredictability of the darkness and the creative magic that can be found there.

The Holly King is a complicated figure, both ominous and protective, and his duality is reflected in the nature of Yule itself. It is the longest night, which perforce means that every night thereafter will be shorter and day longer . . . and yet it is also the start of winter, when those days are coldest and more forbidding.

The Holly King's multidimensional powers can be found in the plants that remain steadfast during the winter months, and we can take inspiration from what they have to offer us.

Holly

The lord of winter's namesake isn't a towering fir, but a mere shrub—and yet there is nothing meek about holly. Its leaves are sharp and sturdy, and its poisonous berries are bloodred. Holly warns any who might dare approach that they are likely to regret it, and yet within holly's embrace that same fierceness becomes a safe space. Holly is renowned for its protection magic, which offers shelter against any harm. It is also healing, in the way that rest can be healing—you can trust holly to take care of you when you aren't feeling your best. Holly will also invite love and creativity, guarding and comforting you while you dream and explore new possibilities in your life and relationships.

Mistletoe

We think of mistletoe as the romantic winter plant, sneakily hung over doorways to catch unsuspecting lovers, as if mistletoe had watched way too many rom-coms and lives only for the meet-cute. But mistletoe has its own dark history. Back when the world was young, Odin and Frigga, rulers of the Norse gods, had many sons, including Baldr, the god of light, joy, purity, and hope. His mother feared for his life and called upon all the plants of the forest to vow never to harm him . . . but she overlooked the humble mistletoe, so quiet and harmless it seemed to be. It will shock no one familiar with Norse mythology that Loki, the god of mischief, didn't particularly care for this brother, and so he tricked Hod, the blind god of darkness and winter, into shooting an arrow made of mistletoe—which went through Baldr's heart. Because of Loki's jealousy, Baldr was sent to the underworld . . . and yet his light remained for half of the year. Despite this tragedy, mistletoe was revered for the lessons it taught. If enemy warriors met beneath mistletoe in the forest, they had to lay down their arms, and mistletoe was hung in the rafters on feast days to prevent disputes.

It is heartwarming to think of the journey mistletoe has undergone, moving from tragedy and darkness into joy, playfulness, and romance. Winter can be a time of transformation, and perhaps mistletoe, with all its protection, love, and creativity magic, can inspire us to find a new way of being, with more joy and love.

Pine

The pine tree is sacred to a number of deities from cultures all over the world, but the story that best reveals its true nature is that of Pitys and Pan. Pitys was a nymph, while Pan was the satyr god of the wild. As is common in Greek mythology, Pan sought Pitys's affections, and when she refused, he chased her across the mountains. She ran and ran, but he was faster than she was. Just as he was about to catch her, she prayed to the gods for their help—and they turned her into a pine tree—so strong that despite Pan's attempts to chop it down, it stood resolute. In fact, it is said that Pitys's pine still stands on the mountainside, safe and self-sufficient, despite the calls or even attacks of the wild. By no means should we *always* be a tree, unmovable and unchanging. The wild is a source of creativity and adventure . . . but we do need rest, and our creativity should come on our own terms. Pine reminds us that we are our own source of strength, and that we can set our own boundaries and make our own choices.

Rosemary

In ancient Greece, students would wear rosemary garlands around their necks to help them retain their lessons, and this association has carried on since then, through Ophelia telling Hamlet, "There's rosemary, that's for remembrance," and on into today. Perhaps it is rosemary's strong scent that has given it this connection with memory; after all, scent and memory are deeply tied to one another, and rosemary's fragrance lingers in the air. It may also be because of rosemary's evergreen nature, allowing us to remember the summer even in the depths of winter.

Yew

The yew is sacred to Morrigan, the Celtic goddess of death. She has black hair and eyes and wears a cloak made of ravens. Perhaps Morrigan is the reason the yew is known as the tree of the dead; it serves as a portal through which the dead can journey to their rest. And yet yew trees themselves rarely die; if conditions are right, they can live for thousands of years. They grow off of one another, as fallen branches of the elders sprout new life. Yew trees remind us that death can also be a beginning—so when it feels like something has to come to an end, whether it's a relationship, a career path, a friendship, or a dream you once had, it is all right to let it fall, trusting that something new will emerge from it. Yew is farsighted—which is why it's often used for prophesying—and can see all the possibilities that lie ahead, even when you feel that, right now, there is only darkness.

YULE RITUAL TO FIND LIGHT IN THE DARKNESS

Yule is not a night to be spent alone in contemplation; it is a time for celebration, for finding joy in those we love. That doesn't have to mean family or romantic partners—and it doesn't have to mean celebration in person. Yule is simply an opportunity to *reach out* to others, embracing our connections, whatever that means to you.

If you're able to do so, invite some of those treasured people to come and celebrate, either physically or virtually. Like all of the sabbats, Yule is a party! Here are some ways to prepare:

Brew up some mulled wine by heating a bottle of red wine and adding a quarter cup or so of brandy. When it is steaming but not quite simmering, add the following:

- **CINNAMON** for protection, prosperity, intuition, healing, and love

- **HONEY** for creativity, protection, love, and healing

- **ORANGE PEEL** for protection, prosperity, love, creativity, and joy

- **STAR ANISE** for protection, creativity, healing, love, abundance, and divination

Weave a wreath made of whatever flexible plants are available to you, particularly yew, pine, mistletoe, and holly. It doesn't have to be perfect; it just needs to hold together enough to nestle a white pillar candle within it. At some point in the night, every celebrant should find a quiet moment to take a piece of paper and write down an intention they want to hold in the coming days of dark and cold. Set that paper aflame, letting the light carry it in the darkness.

Choose a traditional yule log; rather than the cake, this will be a large chunk of wood.

- If you have a fireplace or the ability to make a fire outside, build up your "bonfire," but wait to add your yule log until it's really roaring. Before you do so, pour a libation of mulled wine over it, along with some drops of honey and a sprinkle of rosemary. Burn it in honor of the Holly King, but be sure to save a piece of your yule log, carefully fishing it out of the fire. Store it in a safe place, and then use it to start your Yule fire next year.

- If you do not have a fireplace, use your yule log as an altar. You can nestle pine cones, holly sprigs, yewberries, and mistletoe within its nooks and crannies. You can arrange crystals associated with Yule like bloodstone, blue topaz, and clear quartz atop it, adding any objects that, for you, represent the opposing forces of wildness and protection. If you like, you can invite others to add their own objects to the Yule altar.

Say farewell to the sun as it sets, knowing that this will be the longest period of time you will be apart . . . and then, embrace the darkness. Light candles and fill the quiet with laughter as you share good food and good company. Wassailing, a secular form of caroling, is traditional, so you might consider singing songs like "The Holly and the Ivy," or you could sing your favorite pop tunes—it's not so much about *what* you sing, but *why*. You're singing for the joy of it, for the pleasure of hearing your voice entwined with the voices of those you love.

Week Five

THE LIGHT OF THE DECEMBER MOON

As the winter solstice falls in December, the full moon of this month is known as the Long Night Moon, as well as the Cold Moon. The moon of the longest night shines for a greater period of time than any other; so ironically, there is more moonlight in greater darkness.

What can you see about yourself in the light of this moon? What hides in your own darkness, whether it's an emotion you've been wanting to avoid or a troubling pattern you've found yourself caught in?

Suggested Spell

For a moment, let yourself really *feel* the cold of the December moon. Step outside without gloves, hat, or jacket, just long enough to allow the chill to reach your bones. We talk about the value of warmth, but cold has its indispensable qualities as well—it offers us clarity, the ability to see things sharply—just as they are in all their truth.

Bring something from the cold back into the warmth with you. If there's snow, gather it in a jar, or perhaps take a lone stick or rock that is lying on the ground. Sleep with it beside you, and allow its wintry insight to guide your dreams.

Week Six

NEW MOON IN SAGITTARIUS

When the new moon ventures into daring and imaginative Sagittarius, prepare yourself for new adventures. The old patterns that have been revealing themselves to you this month are about to loosen their grip, allowing space for initiations, new beginnings, and novel experiences.

Suggested Spell

Take a piece of paper and write down one thing that feels entirely out of character for you . . . and yet is something you would very much like to embody. It might be a hobby you have never tried or an intention to start a friendship or even just to speak your mind more often. Light a candle to harness the fiery nature of Sagittarius, and nearby, place an agate crystal to invite courage, strength, and confidence, as well as mookaite, known as the stone of adventure. Fold your paper in a multiple of three, then set it aflame. Place it on a plate to capture its ashes—and for safety, of course! When it's burned away entirely, take the ashes outside. Use your breath to cast them into the wind with all its possibilities.

Week Seven

SUN IN CAPRICORN

Most of the time, we don't have the energy to do the grunt work necessary to fulfill our dreams. This isn't to say we don't work toward them—of course we do, all the time—but it can be difficult to force ourselves to do the more tedious tasks, the ones that require organization and patience. But when the sun is in Capricorn, we are filled with practicality.

We are feeling the impetus to go through that to-do list and take joy in crossing things off.

Suggested Spell

To support this Capricorn energy, perform this task-mastering spell. You'll need a piece of paper and a pen, a bowl of water, a jar, and peppermint, tea tree, and lemon essential oils.

Write down every task you've been avoiding. Don't stint—include the ones that don't even seem all that urgent, as well as the ones that have been keeping you up at night. Without folding the paper, place it in the bowl of water. As it softens, press the edges down so that it is entirely submerged.

Sprinkle three drops of peppermint essential oil into the water while speaking your intention for success aloud or silently.

Sprinkle three drops of tea tree essential oil while speaking your intention for practicality aloud or silently.

Sprinkle three drops of lemon essential oil while speaking your intention for energy and clear thought aloud or silently.

Seal the water and paper in a jar, and keep it on your altar while the sun is in Capricorn.

Week Eight

FULL MOON IN GEMINI

When the duality of Gemini meets the powerful manifestation magic of the full moon, it means that anything is possible. Ideas that might have felt contradictory can seem more compatible with one another, and conversations with others can spark inspiration and guide you down new paths. Take this energy and allow your intellect to guide you . . . it may lead you in a direction you never would have foreseen.

Suggested Spell

Since Gemini can feel restless and easily distracted and since lunar energy can be unpredictable, it is a good idea to perform a spell for focus. Gather black tourmaline, smoky quartz, or obsidian to help you feel grounded; selenite for clarity; and fluorite to help with concentration. In the light of the full moon, hold each crystal in the open palm of your nondominant hand. Let the moonlight fill your crystal with all that you need, as you hold each one for the space of three inhales and exhales before moving on to the next. When you've finished, place your crystals on your altar or even on your desk to keep their energy close by.

Week Nine

JANUARY MOON

January is the Wolf Moon, and while wolves represent strength and leadership, they also symbolize wilderness and chaos. How can you find that strength of mind within yourself, while also allowing the creative wild to spark? One without the other—leadership without passion, imagination without vitality—leaves us feeling unfulfilled, as if experiencing a life half-lived.

Suggested Spell

What if you were to howl at the moon?

If this feels uncomfortable, or if you live in a place or with people that would find this inappropriate, it absolutely is something you can engage in silently. All you need to do is step outside into the night. Look around you—wherever you are, *this* time in *this* place is *yours*. Right now, this is your territory. Feel your own strength, your own passion. Cast your gaze upward, with your throat exposed to the air. Call out the wild within you, with your voice or simply with your breath and your energy, exhaling your essence. Let the world know that you are there.

Week Ten

NEW MOON IN CAPRICORN

The possibilities that arrive with any new moon are tempered by Capricorn's focus and pragmatism, so while typically new moons are a time for dreaming and anticipation, this particular new moon is best spent getting organized. Clear out the cobwebs, both literally and figuratively, to make space for new growth.

Suggested Spell

In the morning, gather some mint, lemon, or rosemary essential oil. Put a few drops into a bowl and dilute it with a few drops of carrier oil like jojoba or rose hip that are safe for use on the face. Anoint *ajna*, your third eye chakra between your brows, to help you see your next steps clearly without distractions. Close your eyes and inhale deeply, breathing in the clarifying scent. Let your thoughts go by you as you breathe, without trying to catch hold of any of them. Just let them float out and away from you, always coming back to the scent and your breath. When you feel complete—which isn't to say when you have no more thoughts; thoughts will always come and go as they will—open your eyes and begin your day.

Week Eleven

SUN IN AQUARIUS

Aquarius offers the spirit of independence, original thinking, and a commitment to doing good in the world. When the sun is in Aquarius, that creative, world-shifting energy is present in all of us. What will you do with it this week? How will you embrace your own originality and independence to bring about positive change? If you're not an Aquarius and not used to that kind of spark, the pressure of this shift might feel a little overwhelming. Impacting the world creatively sounds like a big responsibility . . . but in truth, even the smallest changes can have an enormous effect. Let your intuition guide you.

Suggested Spell

Gather together your intuition, your creativity, and your personal power in this spell jar. You'll need the following:

* **Opal, lapis lazuli, sugilite, and/or amethyst, for intuition**

* **Holly, calendula, mugwort, and/or wormwood, for intuition**

* **Garnet and/or carnelian, for creativity**

* **Basil, ginger, and/or vervain, for creativity**

* **Agate, bloodstone, tigereye, and/or red jasper, for personal power**

* **Garlic, yarrow, cinnamon, and/or orange peels, for personal power**

Layer the ingredients in a small glass jar in the order listed. If you have a specific intention in mind for what you want to do this week, write it on a piece of paper and place it in the jar. Seal it tight, and keep the jar nearby as an inspiring force to help you take one big (or one small) step toward positive change, both in your life and in the world.

Week Twelve

FULL MOON IN CANCER

As the most emotional constellation of the horoscope, Cancer always tends to be full of feelings, but the moon is also its luminary, making it more powerful than ever this week. This might feel intense, but it's also an opportunity. The full moon brings to light all of the emotions you've been keeping hidden . . . but it only reveals them to *you*. Self-knowledge is a powerful thing, for it is only when we know and allow ourselves to experience all that we feel that we can understand how to move forward.

Suggested Spell

Gather the following crystals:

* **Malachite, which helps to release and soothe stored emotions**

* **Moonstone, which encourages inner peace and harmony**

* **Rhodochrosite, which helps heal emotional wounds**

* **Rose quartz, to encourage self-love**

Place the clean rose quartz and moonstone in a small bowl of water, nestling the malachite and rhodochrosite beside them. (Don't immerse the malachite and rhodochrosite—they might dissolve.) Allow the crystals to rest in the light of the full moon to charge them with lunar energy. Before you go to sleep, dip your fingertips in the water, and rub a little of it over your heart. You can also anoint yourself in any place that feels a little tender. Take care of yourself.

IMBOLC

February 1

I MBOLC OCCURS AT THE MIDPOINT BETWEEN THE WINTER solstice and the spring equinox, so while the length of the night is not yet equal to that of the day, it is steadily waning. With that growing light comes the burgeoning of life—most trees do not yet have leaves, but the birch and elm are beginning to bud, and at their feet grow the crocuses, hellebore, and snowdrops that herald the coming spring.

Imbolc also suggests that the winter's rest is coming to an end. Lambs are beginning to quicken, and the pastures must be tended to ready them for the livestock that will soon be wandering.

Also known as St. Brigid's Day, Imbolc is dedicated to the Celtic goddess Brigid. Kildare Abbey, or Cill-Dara for "Church of the Oak," was named for an oak tree that was sacred to Brigid, and it was there that her worshippers would light a fire on Imbolc. Though Kildare Abbey burned down in the twelfth century, on that same hill now stands Kildare Cathedral, and in 1993, that flame for Brigid was relit by Sister Mary Teresa Cullen of the Brigidine Sisters. It continues to burn eternally today. Incidentally, Kildare Cathedral also features a sheela na gig, a carving of a naked woman displaying her vulva. Theories as to the meaning of this figure run through the typical warding off of lustful impulses, but as the carvings of sheela na gigs tend to be older than the buildings they have been incorporated into, it is more likely that they are holdovers from older faiths that celebrated feminine power.

Brigid is the daughter of Dagda, an earth god of the Tuatha Dé Danann, a legendary folk who have inspired tales of the fae and of elves. She watches over the cattle in the fields, preventing them from getting lost, and is a goddess not only of agriculture, but of creativity, music, healing, motherhood, poetry, and the sacred feminine. She often appeared as a red-headed goddess with a cloak made of sunbeams, and she kept her own domesticated animals, including the oxen Fe and Men; Torc Triath, the king of boars; and Cirb, the king of sheep.

When the Tuatha Dé Danann battled against the original people of Ireland, they fought vicious giants called the Fomorians. They won, but Dagda, Brigid's father, was mortally wounded and died on the journey home, and Brigid's son Ruadán was killed in battle against Goibhniu, the smith god. When Ruadán fell, Brigid rushed to his side and gave a crying lament—and thus, on the first day that Ireland experienced sadness, the tradition of women keening at gravesides began. Keens are not songs; they do not contain lyrics or melody—they are raw, unearthly emotion, and because a keen is dedicated to the person who has died, it is never to be repeated.

Brigid's legends are often similar in tone to those of fairy tales; when asked for her blessing, she would grant it only to those who were pure of heart. For instance, when encountering a beggar in the countryside, Brigid offered him her own ragged cloak, but when she laid it across his shoulders, it transformed into a shimmering cloak of pure white, providing warmth and protection to any who wore it. (In a related tale, St. Brigid claimed land for Kildare from the king of Leinster by throwing this same cloak on the ground, covering far more ground than any could have believed possible.)

However, if the supplicant was not worthy, Brigid would cause them to undergo a trial that would teach them a lesson. When encountering another beggar (Brigid's legends often feature beggars) who came to her doorstep cold and hungry, she offered him use of her magical white cow, which could produce an unlimited supply of milk. She told him, though, to take excellent care of the cow and treat her with the utmost respect, and of course to share what he had with others. As these stories go, at first the beggar obeyed, but before long he became greedy and hoarded the milk for himself. Brigid confronted him, but instead of being wrathful, she offered him a way to earn her forgiveness: he must visit every house in the village, offering the cow's nourishment to all—and like Strega Nona's pasta pot, the cow never ran dry.

Brigid wasn't interested in punishment, but in teaching him to become more compassionate. Brigid helped people be better.

CLOOTIE WELLS

Brigid also served as a kind of water goddess, as she is associated with healing wells known as "clootie wells." These freshwater springs often form tiny ponds at the base of trees, and a cloth wet with their waters could be used to heal any injury. After the injury had been bathed, the clootie cloth would be tied to a branch of the tree, and a small offering would be left at an altar below.

We rely on wells for so many things—they are sources of water from deep within the earth and carry with them trace elements of magnesium, calcium, iron, and manganese, which are medicinally healing, in addition to being spiritually so. Beyond that, these waters carry the memory of the rocks they have flowed through, with all their secrets and stories. Water is changeable, but it is also everlasting, recycling itself over and over from one form to another, but always retaining the same composition.

If we could plumb the depths of our own wells, what secrets would we find there? Or, put another way, if you were to encounter Brigid at the crossroads, what test would she put you to? How would she encourage you to grow, to heal, to become better?

IMBOLC RITUAL FOR GROWTH AND HEALING

Begin by crafting a besom—a small handmade broom. You'll need a fairly straight and sturdy stick or branch, of oak if possible. Gather some flexible reeds or straw and secure them to the branch with twine. Cover the twine with ribbon—you might consider using white (for purity and the return of light), yellow (for the sun, warmth, and energy), or light green (for new growth and renewal), as they are all sacred to Imbolc. Tuck in some basil, bay laurel, Saint-John's-wort, or meadowsweet. When it's finished, use your besom to sweep out the corners of your home, clearing away any cobwebs, both literal and figurative, that may have collected there over Yuletide. When you've finished, hang your besom (free of any cobwebs) above your doorway or over your altar.

Use your remaining straw to create a Brigid's cross.

Cut the pieces of straw to a uniform length, around twelve to eighteen inches.

Begin by creating an X-shape with two straws, then fold one in half over the other. Rotate the cross ninety degrees, then add another straw, folding it in half and interlocking it with the first folded straw. Continue to repeat this pattern, folding the straws across and under each other. With each fold, set an intention for what you want to release as well as what you want to cultivate in the coming warmth.

Once you've reached the size you want, secure the straws with twine, and hang your cross with some ribbon to invite Brigid's blessing.

Now that you've made your home ready for new growth, it's time to venture out to a clootie well—or a metaphorical one, at any rate. All that's really required in this instance is wild water, which means it has been collected by some means untouched by machinery. You might visit a spring if there is one nearby or a river, lake, or pond. If it's raining, you might place a bowl out to catch new-formed water from the sky. If you're in a place where you can perform a clootie ritual without feeling self-conscious, that's wonderful, but if not, simply scoop some water up in a glass jar, seal it, and bring it home with you.

Choose your cloth with intention. It doesn't need to be anything fancy; most clootie cloths are in the form of rags. But it does need to have meaning to you. You can tear a scrap from a beloved but now stained T-shirt or use a piece of a dishcloth that has dried many dishes and wiped up many spills. Dip your cloth in the water. Is there a part of your body that could use its healing? (Be mindful, of course, that pond or river water and open wounds do not mix well.) Perhaps you have a bruise on your knee or a bruise on your heart. When you've finished, wring out the cloth and tie it to a tree. Let it dry there in the breeze, and add a small offering to the water in the form of a stone you've found. As you drop it in, give thanks to Brigid as well as the lessons life has for us all.

And then, toward the end of the day, light a fire! This can be as big as a bonfire or as small as a single candle—as always, intention is all that is needed here. If it's a larger fire, scatter some basil, rosemary, bay laurel, chamomile, Saint-John's-wort, and/or lavender into the flames. If you're using a candle, anoint the sides of the candle with any of the above essential oils that are available to you. Inhale their scent and watch the flames flicker, and if it feels right, you might consider the following incantation:

By your healing touch, gracious Brigid.
Mend our wounds and lift what's frigid.
Grant us strength, renewal, and grace.
In your light we find our place.

Week Thirteen

FEBRUARY MOON

February's moon has a variety of names—the Snow Moon, the Hunger Moon, and the Storm Moon—and all of them are fairly bleak and turbulent. On the Gregorian calendar, February is the shortest month, but of course, its lunar cycle is the same length as any other. The difficulty with February is that we *know* winter is nearing its end, but it doesn't *feel* that way, not yet. The harsh winds still blow, the snow still falls and lies on the ground, dirty and stripped of its luster. We are hungry for new growth and sunshine and must turn to our inner resilience, our internal stores of light and warmth, to see us through.

Suggested Spell

Gather some frozen water—maybe it's snow from outside if that's around where you live, or it can even be ice from your freezer. Place it in a bowl and add some or all of the following crystals:

* **Amethyst, for emotional balance and growth**

* **Black tourmaline, for grounding and to shield from negative energy**

* **Blue lace agate, for soothing calm**

* **Carnelian, for warmth and vitality**

* **Clear quartz, for calm and balance**

Light a blue or white candle, and place it next to the bowl. Take a piece of paper and write down any challenges you might be struggling with this week. Below that, write the following:

> *Beneath the storm, I stand strong,*
> *Resilience within, a spirit unyielding.*

You can also write whatever incantation feels most supportive for you. Place the paper atop the crystals, over the ice. Let it rest there until it becomes damp all the way through, infusing your intention with resilience, strength, and adaptability. Lifting it up before the words dissolve, carefully hold it near the candle flame so that it feels the heat but does not catch fire. Once the paper has dried, add it to your altar to see you through February, removing and drying your crystals before disposing of the water.

Week Fourteen

NEW MOON IN AQUARIUS

This new moon brings a sense of mystery and possibility to the already creative and adaptable Aquarius. This week you may want to consider your own ability to embrace change, knowing that whatever changes do come your way—or that you make for yourself—will be beneficial not only to you, but to those in your community as well. The shifts that are coming are positive ones, but they may be startling all the same, particularly as they are likely to be unexpected.

Suggested Spell

Harness Aquarius's partnership with the element of air by making a wish on it. Air is a powerful force for putting an intention out into the world. At some point in our lives, we've all made a wish and blown on a dandelion clock, releasing its seeds into the breeze. We make a wish when we blow out birthday candles, and each time we do, we cast a spell.

In this case, you may want to consider focusing your spell on allowing for the possibilities to come, whatever they look like. You might walk outside, breathing in the sharp February air, and collect dried leaves. When you have a handful, crumble them in your hands, and as you do, scatter them into the air. It doesn't matter if the wind is blowing hard or not—the air will carry your intentions.

Week Fifteen

SUN IN PISCES

Pisces is the dreamiest of the signs, combining creativity with empathy in a way that allows the imagination to become manifest, generating new ways of being in the world. The energy of the sun amplifies all of this, inviting warmth and sensitivity. Let yourself be dreamy this week, as daydreams can inspire us to consider what might actually be possible in reality.

Suggested Spell

Take a cleansing bath just before bed to invite powerful dreams. If you have a bathtub, that's great, but you can also simply use a large bowl. Heat some water, then add the following fresh or dried herbs:

* **Lavender, for peace and calm**

* **Lemon balm, for lightness and joy**

* **Sage, for wisdom**

Not all crystals can be submerged in water without damage, but if they're available, add citrine to invite the energy of the sun and aventurine to set the intention for playful and intrepid dreams. Immerse yourself, including the crown of your head, in your bath, or simply pour the bowl of ritual water over your head, dowsing yourself in its dreamy warmth. When you've finished, don't rinse off. Pat yourself dry, leaving the power of your spell bath in place.

Week Sixteen

FULL MOON IN LEO

The moon is a force for chaotic, emotional energy, so a full moon in Leo can manifest a lot of drama. That's not necessarily a bad thing! We think of drama as equating to *melodrama*—which is when someone overreacts or is excessively emotional, or when a situation seems that way. But drama can also just mean powerful or intense, and not excessively or falsely so. Something that is intense doesn't always feel good, and often drama does come with conflict in one form or another—interpersonal or internal—but it's usually caused by underlying circumstances. There's a *reason* for drama, whether it's long-held resentments or powerful emotions.

Suggested Spell

Lunar scrying allows you to use the light of the full moon to uncover what might be causing any intensity you might be experiencing. On the night when the moon is full, fill a bowl with water, and if it's possible to do so, place the bowl so that the moonlight shines down into it. Light a candle and let its light flicker over the water as well.

Lean over the bowl and peer into it, letting your breath disturb the surface and make the candle dance. Your reflection will be distorted—what does that fuzziness allow you to see within?

OSTARA

March 21

O STARA FALLS ON THE SPRING EQUINOX, THE MIDPOINT between the height of winter and the height of summer. The length of the day is equal to the length of the night, as everything is held perfectly in balance. Ostara feels like a held breath, a moment of tension—a fulcrum just about to tip over into the ease of the coming summer's warmth.

As Ostara is the acknowledged first day of spring, with its coming, life begins to truly burst forth from the cold ground. The alder and ash trees begin to unfurl their leaves, and the delicate cherry blossoms begin to send their fragrance into the clean, crisp air. Daffodils wave in the breeze, their buttery color a warm note of cheerful welcome even when the day is gray.

Ostara is named for Eostre, a Germanic goddess of the dawn, fertility, and the spring season. Not much is known about her, and it is possible that she is an amalgamation of a variety of goddesses, including Freya, the Norse goddess of love, beauty, fertility, and resurrection. But she is described by Jacob Grimm in *Deutsche Mythologie* as being the etymological and mythological root of Easter feasts, so if you've ever wondered why eggs play such an important role in celebrating Easter, the answer lies in legends of Eostre.

Eostre is often depicted as a young and radiant goddess, lit from within by the dawn. As with any Disney princess, the wild creatures gathered around her, and birds would alight upon her fingertips. She sent these birds out as heralds of the spring, the swallows and robins returning north and bringing her warmth with them.

Unfortunately, one of her messengers was injured in flight, and Eostre came upon him lying on the ground, dying. She took the bird in her hands and transformed it into a hare—swift, hardy, and plentiful, able to spread the life Eostre offers the world with more ease and safety than a bird could.

And yet, the transformation was not quite complete. Unlike most Leporidae—or mammals, for that matter—this particular hare retained the ability to lay eggs, scattering brightly colored orbs across the land in celebration of spring.

Certain birds have more precise meanings, of course—crows represent darkness and owls represent wisdom. But the bird in Eostre's story is never specified; it is simply a bird, tossed about the waning winter winds. Birds are often depicted as messengers, as this one was, but they also symbolize delicacy, independence, and spirituality. They can fly, which gives them greater freedom than we landbound folk will ever know, but as they are also small and hollow-boned, with their gift of flight comes the cost of vulnerability. But their literally higher perspective allows them to see more clearly, with more insight and a greater understanding of the full picture than we possess.

When Eostre saved the bird, she did so by sacrificing its power of flight. It can no longer soar above it all, but instead remains grounded. And yet, the hare is still independent—running faster than its predators—and is stronger and safer as well. Hares are often depicted in legends of fertility and rebirth as well as transformation—they are always shifting in and out of their shape as well as their place in this reality. They are intuitive and sensitive, and often a bit tricksy, as well. They are survivors.

Eostre's creature manages to be both at the same time—an intuitive, cunning survivor who retains the memory of flight with all the wider understanding that allows.

OSTARA RITUAL TO FIND BALANCE

In honor of Eostre, begin this day with the dawn. Rise early to greet her warming light, and brew yourself a cup of tea. You'll need a teaspoon's worth of some mixture of the following dried herbs:

* **Chamomile**
* **Lavender**
* **Lemon balm**
* **Nettle**
* **Rose**

Each of these plants is soothing and loving, helping you to find peace. Add them to a strainer and pour just-boiled water over them, allowing them to steep, covered, for at least five minutes. Add some milk and honey, and sip your tea beside a window where you can watch the dark of night brighten with the dawn.

When you're ready to begin your day, go out in search of the signs of spring. You might gather newly budded leaves and some enterprising wildflowers. Look for daffodils, apple and cherry blossoms, cyclamen and gorse. Place them in a basket or, if you like, in the folds of your skirts, and bring them home with you. Place them in your windowsills, scatter them across your table—invite spring indoors, with all its warmth and energy.

And, of course, color some eggs! Many of us grew up on the regular old supermarket egg-dyeing kits, but there are many other ways to experiment with invoking that first egg-laying rabbit. They may not be as brightly colored, but they will carry your intentions farther.

Before you start, sketch a simplified symbol of the balance of Ostara: the bird/hare. It doesn't have to be perfect or beautiful; in fact, the simpler the better. When you're ready, take a white crayon and draw your design onto some or all of your hard-boiled eggs, focusing your thoughts on the areas in which you want to achieve balance in your own life. Where do you need to be grounded? Where do you need to soar?

At the same time, brew several bowls of very strong tea:

* **Black tea, for a reddish-brown**

* **Butterfly pea flower, for a light blue**

* **Hibiscus tea, for a dusty gray**

* **Red rooibos tea, for orange**

* **Tumeric tea, for a golden color**

You'll want three bags of each type of tea for every two cups of water—then let them steep until they reach room temperature. Add a tablespoon of white vinegar to each mixture, then add four eggs maximum to each color. Let them set for six hours in the refrigerator.

Water, of course, is already a part of your dyeing process, but if you like, you can incorporate the remaining elements, too:

EARTH. Add a pinch of soil to the dye, inviting grounding and stability.

AIR. Blow on the eggs as you place them in the dyebath, adding your spirit and your voice.

FIRE. You might light a candle and briefly hold each egg over the flame, invoking its creative powers.

While the eggs are dyeing, do a little spring cleaning, working around the flowers and plants you have placed around your home. Tidy everything away, give the floor a good sweep, and air out all that might have grown stagnant over the winter months.

Fill a medium-sized bowl with water and add a few handfuls of the plants you have collected, placing them in the water one at a time. As you do so, you might consider the following invocation:

Eostre, goddess of spring's rebirth
In your essence, balance finds its worth.
As light and dark dance in unity,
I find harmony and serenity.

Cradle the bowl gently in your arms and walk around your space, dipping your fingers into the water and flicking them, cleansing and reviving your home with the flowers' essence.

When the eggs are ready, give some thought to how you want to work with them. Hiding them is not only traditional, but also deeply magical—and it's harder than it seems like it ought to be. (Please note—you definitely don't need to have or be a child to enjoy this!) The act of placing each egg is a strategic and intentional practice: *Who do you think will find this egg? What do they tend to look for? What will they experience when they find it? Is placing it in this particular nook meaningful in some way?*

And there is always something magical about *finding* eggs, too. Even if we know they've been hidden for us, questions arise: *Who did the hiding? Where would they choose? What messages were they trying to send? Where have I not yet considered?*

You can hide them again and again, looking for new places to surprise each other.

There is always the question of what exactly to do with so very many hard-boiled eggs, beautiful as they may be. There are the usual deviled eggs and egg salad, both of which are delicious. But if you want something a little lighter, and a little more spring-y, if you will, consider the following:

Enchanting Spring Salad with Herb Blessing

Ingredients for the Salad

2 tablespoons lemon juice

2 tablespoons olive oil

salt and pepper, to taste

2 cups mixed spring greens

1 cup sugar snap peas, trimmed

1 cup cherry tomatoes, halved

½ cup radishes, thinly sliced

4 hard-boiled eggs, peeled and sliced

Ingredients for the Herb Blessing

fresh herbs

honey

apple cider vinegar

salt

Gather a small handful of fresh herbs, including basil, chamomile, mint, and thyme. Cup them in your palms, and feel their energy mix with yours. Add them to a mortar and gently crush them with a pestle, releasing their juices and blending them together. Stir in a tablespoon of honey and a tablespoon of apple cider vinegar, as well as a pinch of salt. Incorporate your intentions for nourishment, renewal, and balance.

For the Salad

Add the lemon juice and olive oil to a large bowl and whisk them together, along with salt and pepper to taste. Add the fresh ingredients to the bowl and gently mix them with your hands, coating everything with the dressing. Dot the salad with the egg slices, placing each egg with intention and recognition of the transformative powers of Ostara. Sprinkle the Herb Blessing over the top as a final step, then serve this salad as a sacred dish, allowing its vibrant colors and magical ingredients to nourish your body and spirit. With each bite, savor the flavors and embrace the energy of renewal and balance.

Week Seventeen

MARCH MOON

The March full moon is known as the Worm Moon, which can be off-putting until you consider the meaning behind it. This is the month when the worms begin to wake up, emerging from their deeper burrows and moving through the upper layers of soil. They engage with the roots of plants, awakening them from their own dormancy. The newly arrived robins begin pecking at the ground, tugging up those worms as they work to build their nests. The March moon is a time for activity, for beginning the hard work of growth in the warming year.

Suggested Spell

Break your own new ground by digging your hands into the soil. You may be tempted to do this without gloves, but depending on where you are, the ground may be quite hard and/or contaminated, so check out your surroundings before deciding whether to use gloves or not—they won't impact the power of your spell. Bring a jar outside and wander around for a bit before starting to dig. Choose a spot that feels open and free, full of potential. Kneel down in the dirt and use your hands to loosen the soil, pulling up clumps with your fingers and adding them to your jar. When it's just about full, seal it up. When you're back home, take a slip of paper and write down what you wish to accomplish during this lunar cycle. Fold it up tight and add it to your jar, shaking the earth around so that the paper is fully coated. The work has begun.

Week Eighteen

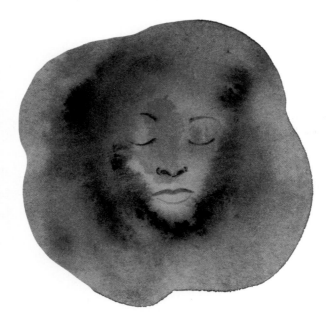

NEW MOON IN PISCES

When the intuition and sensitivity of Pisces are held in shadow during the new moon, it actually becomes easier to see the things we miss in the blinding light of day. We are better able to connect with *ajna*, the third eye chakra, the source of our intuition and inner sight.

Suggested Spell

Find a quiet and peaceful space where you can comfortably sit or lie down, and ensure that you have an amethyst, lapis lazuli, sodalite, fluorite, azurite, labradorite, or other crystal that resonates with the third eye chakra.

Take three deep breaths, closing your eyes and visualizing a vibrant indigo light glowing at the center of your forehead, just above your brows. Place your stone right on this chakra, holding it in place, feeling the cool crystal come into resonance with your body temperature. Let its energy mingle with yours.

Remain there, breathing, for as long as you like, allowing any insights to arise as they will. When you feel complete, let your hands rest in your lap, cupping the crystal in your open palms. Open your eyes slowly, permitting external reality to meld with your internal reality.

Week Nineteen

SUN IN ARIES

Without question, this is a powerful time. Aries is the fieriest of signs, and when its luminary, the orb of fire in the sky, is fully aligned, we all feel our strength and inner fire rise. We are more self-confident and better able to access the courage needed to live fully as ourselves in all our authenticity and power. When the sun is in Aries, it's time to explore your own passions, assert your needs, and discover more about who you are at your burning core.

Suggested Spell

Go outdoors at solar noon, when the sun is at its zenith. (You'll likely need to look up precisely what time this will be in your exact location.) Spread your arms wide and tilt your face up to the sun—it's there, even if it's hidden behind clouds. *Take up space.* Be yourself in all that you are. If you want to, spin around until you get dizzy. Shout. Feel the fullness of you, brave and loud and brimming with fire. Take this moment and hold on to it, carrying it with you so you can always access it whenever you need it.

Week Twenty

FULL MOON IN VIRGO

The full moon in Virgo has much the same meaning as a Worm Moon—
they are both grounded, practical, and hardworking—and so when the
full moon in Virgo falls during the Worm Moon, their shared energy is
amplified exponentially. All that hard work becomes even more focused
and detail-oriented, and often is directed outward—Virgo is kind and
longs to be of service, and you can use that push to give back to the world
around you.

Suggested Spell

All that outward-focused work can be draining, however, and so the suggested spell this week is one of self-care. On the night of the full moon,
pour a soothing oil like jojoba or sweet almond into a small bowl. Add
some combination of the following essential oils, making sure it smells
good to you:

* **Cedarwood, for balance and stability**

* **Eucalyptus, for purification**

* **Frankincense, for grounding**

* **Lavender, for calm**

* **Lemon, for energy**

* **Peppermint, for clarity**

Dip your fingers into the oil, mixing the scents together, and then use it to perform a gentle self-massage, lovingly rubbing the oil into your hands and wrists as well as the soles of your feet and anywhere else that needs tending. Take your time, and work to remind yourself that you, too, deserve love and care.

Week Twenty-One

APRIL MOON

The Pink Moon of April receives its name from the phlox flower—clusters of small, star-shaped blossoms with delicate, charming ruffles at the edges, like little petticoats. Their sweet fragrance attracts bees as well as the butterflies that have recently emerged from their cocoons.

In a way, April is very similar to this transformation—its moon, also known as the Breaking Ice Moon, is a time when the rivers begin to run freely, and we find our flow.

Suggested Spell

Place a few ice cubes in a bowl, along with a clear quartz crystal. (Clear quartz is safe in salt water, but not all crystals are.) Note the ways in which the crystal differs from the ice, as well as the ways in which they

are the same. Take a pinch of salt and sprinkle it over the ice. As you do so, visualize breaking free of anything that's been holding you back. Take another pinch and sprinkle again, then once more, each time envisioning your release.

Peer into the bowl. Note how the salt pits the ice, causing it to come apart and melt more quickly. Inhale deeply in this gentle, eyes-open meditation, watching the slow transformation of solid into liquid, frozen into free-flowing. When the clear quartz is all that remains in the salt water, remove it and dry it off without rinsing it. Keep it close by you this month, as a reminder that you, too, are free and clear.

Week Twenty-Two

NEW MOON IN ARIES

When the new moon is in Aries, it's time to release your anger. Aries tends to be hot-tempered, but when that energy is soothed by the infinite possibilities of the new moon, there is space to let go of old hurts and resentments. This can mean forgiveness, but it doesn't have to—all that's really needed or wanted here is a little space from that anger. Sometimes, a little distance can provide the opportunity to see differently, to feel differently . . . to move differently, onto a new path.

Suggested Spell

On the night of the new moon, gather the following:

* **Two pieces of paper**

* **A pencil**

* **A lit candle**

* **A small bowl**

* **A teaspoon's worth of neutral unscented oil**

* **A feather or a small twig**

On the first piece of paper, write an old resentment. Write out your anger, as well as any other emotions you've been feeling for a long time. Write it all down. Fold up the piece of paper until it will fit in the bowl, then carefully hold it to the flame. Drop it into the bowl and let it burn down completely, until nothing is left but ashes. You may have to lift it to the flame more than once—which is okay!

When the fire is out and the ashes are cool, add a few drops of oil. Use your finger to stir the mixture around until you've made a paste. Add some more oil until you've reached a consistency you can write with.

Take the second piece of paper. Holding the feather or twig as a quill, dip it into the ink you've made of the ashes, and use it to write out a symbol—perhaps a heart, perhaps a star?—of something new. Keep your paper on your altar, beneath your pillow, or in your pocket.

Week Twenty-Three

SUN IN TAURUS

Taurus is a little contradictory. As an earth sign, it is grounded and practical, focused on stability, security, and perseverance. But Taurus is ruled by Venus, the sensual lover of the zodiac, and can lean into a hedonistic enjoyment of all the pleasures life has to offer. When the sun is in Taurus, it's a time for all of us to look for that paradoxical balance within ourselves.

Suggested Spell

What is something you find deeply pleasurable? Is it stroking a cat, hearing them purr their own pleasure? Is it curling up with a good book on a rainy day? Is it biting into a cookie still warm from the oven or soaking in a hot, scented bubble bath? Whatever it is, do that one thing, but before you get into it, write down all the things that make it *practical*. Yes, it's pleasurable—and that's enough in and of itself!—but what happens on the other side of that pleasurable act? Do you feel safer? Do you feel calmer? There's a common understanding that we must fill our cups so that we can give to others . . . but consider how you are also filling your cup so that it is *full*, and that being happy, safe, and warm is an end in itself. What power and stability can you find in yourself by being full of pleasure? Where is the magic in that?

Week Twenty-Four

FULL MOON IN LIBRA

The season of Ostara is the season of balance, and that remains true when the full moon is in Libra. Symbolized by the scales, Libra is a sign that values balance in all things. Like Taurus, Libra is ruled by Venus, but as an air sign, the pleasure of Venus becomes more of a longing for harmony. Libra is like the breath blown across a flute, finding the perfect resonance of a held note.

Suggested Spell

Do you ever blow across an empty or nearly empty glass bottle? It's a fun experiment, particularly when you fill the bottles with varying amounts of liquid and hear how the sound changes. On the night of the full moon, gather three empty glass bottles, and fill the first until it is approximately one-quarter full. Fill the second until it is

approximately one-eighth full, and leave the third empty. Blow across each of them in turn, creating an arpeggio of breath—it doesn't matter if they don't actually match notes on any known scale. All that matters is that your breath is producing a melody. Use your breath to create harmony, and carry this moment forward into the coming days as you bring harmony to the world around you.

BELTANE

May 1

AS THE MIDPOINT BETWEEN THE SPRING EQUINOX AND the summer solstice, Beltane is the bountiful, glorious height of spring. Bluebells carpet the forest floor while primroses angle their sweet faces up toward the sun. The hawthorn tree (also known as the May Tree) bursts into bloom, its delicate flowers forming little bouquets. Beltane is a joyous, raucous event, with roots in Maiouma, the ancient Greek celebration of Dionysus and Aphrodite. Indeed, it is on this day that the Green Man joins with the May Queen, two figures of folklore who don't quite tie in with their surrounding mythologies.

The Green Man can be linked to Dionysus, as well as Pan and Cernunnos, the Horned God of the Hunt. But he is an entity unto himself and one who can be found in various cultures and folklore throughout history and across the world. Also known as Jack-in-the-Green, he is often depicted as a face made of leaves and vegetation, for he is the embodiment of the connection between humans and the surrounding wild, natural world. He *is* the abundance of spring, full of the vitality that courses through every living thing. But he is also definitively male, a representation of masculine energy in nature. He is wild and untamed, a reminder of our primal connection to the earth. He is a guardian of that wilderness, fierce and protective. But he is also transient—like the spring, he cannot last. His leaves will wither and fade, as he lives the cycle of growth, decay, and rebirth.

The May Queen can also be linked to a variety of deities, including Flora, the Roman goddess of flowers, spring, and fertility; Persephone, the Greek goddess whose return from the underworld heralds the dawn of spring; Freya, the Norse goddess of love, beauty, and fertility; and, of course, Eostre, the goddess of the dawn and Ostara. The May Queen is the feminine counterpart to the Green Man, an allegory of fertility and the blossoming of nature. She wears a crown of flowers, embodying the promise of a bountiful harvest, the growth and vitality of nature in all her abundance. She is often portrayed as a young maiden, fresh with the dew of spring. And indeed, women and girls would often venture into the woods at daybreak on Beltane, collecting dew off of hawthorn blossoms, primroses, and any other wildflowers they could find, bathing themselves in this wild water, and thereby ensuring eternal youth and beauty. Beltane festivals often involve choosing a May Queen from one of these women or girls, who will dress in white, their hair adorned with flowers and ribbons. She will then lead the ritual celebrations, including dancing around a maypole, decorating a May Bough, and, of course, lighting the Beltane bonfires.

The divine hieros gamos (sacred union of deities) between the May Queen and the Green Man is a cosmic marriage, balancing and harmonizing the masculine and feminine energies of nature. Unlike the eternal battle between the Oak King and the Holly King, the May Queen and the Green Man are not opposing forces, but complementary ones. They are interdependent, and when they are joined on Beltane, they bring forth the potential for new life, growth, and the flourishing of nature. The May Queen, as the embodiment of fertility, and the Green Man, as the representation of the life force within nature, come together to ensure the continuation and vitality of the land.

Their marriage is often celebrated through fertility rites. Exchanges of vows, a little woodland frolicking, dancing around a bonfire—these are all traditional ways to invoke the mystical union of the May Queen and the Green Man. The most obvious symbol, the maypole, is actually a fun and surprisingly challenging ritual. The ribbons, associated with the May Queen, entwine themselves around the phallic pole, as the dancers weave in and out, working together to celebrate the cyclical nature of the seasons and the eternal flow of time. The act of dancing around the maypole can bring blessings and protection to the community and to the land, each wrap of the pole building a greater web of connection, fertility, abundance, and good fortune.

The truth is that we all have the Green Man and the May Queen within us, their energies wrapping around our core selves like ribbons on a maypole. Nature is not a gender binary—it is an abundant union that also exists within us, however we may choose to define ourselves—as men, women, or something else.

BELTANE RITUAL TO EXPLORE THE WILDNESS WITHIN

Consider, if you will, how your nature—the wilderness of *you*—can grow and become more fertile, primal, and protective. What can you take away from the hieros gamos of the May Monarch and the Green One? How can you create that same mystical union within yourself, with all the power and magic that could bring? Performing a traditional maypole dance can be a tall order, particularly if you are a solitary witch or mage, or however you think of yourself, or if your coven is geographically distant. But you can evoke that binding of masculine and feminine energies all on your own.

Start by choosing a sturdy branch—for this ritual it will serve as both maypole and May Bough. A hawthorn branch is ideal, if one grows near you, but you could use any tree, as they are all sacred to the May Queen and the Green Man. Secure your branch to the earth by either digging a hole or placing it in a container and surrounding it with sand or dirt. You could even use a Christmas tree stand—anything that will keep the branch upright will do.

The night before your ritual, brew a batch of Maiwein or May Wine. You can do this using a bottle of light white wine or some fresh fruit juice or iced herbal tea. Pour the liquid into a glass jar and add whichever of the following are available to you:

* **Chamomile, for peace and healing**

* **Elderflower, for purification, beauty, and transformation**

* **Lemon balm, for happiness and vitality**

* **Meadowsweet, for love, fertility, protection, and spiritual connection**

* **A sliced lemon, for uplift**

* **A sliced orange, for creativity**

* **Honey to taste, for joy, healing, and longevity**

Stir well, and allow your Maiwein to steep overnight. In the morning, strain out the herbs and citrus, and chill until you're ready to consume.

On the morning of Beltane, go in search of wildflowers. As you wander, dip the tip of your finger into any dew that has collected in a flower that you find, sparkling in the early light, and anoint yourself with it. You might use one drop for your third eye between your brows, smoothing the water in a counterclockwise or widdershins movement to help you see the unseen. You might smear a little over your eyelids to help you better understand what you do see. You might anoint the base of your throat, the space above your heart, your cheeks, or your brow, blessing yourself with all that nature has to offer.

Gather flowers for the May Queen and leaves for the Green Man, bringing them home with you. Sprinkle a few petals and leaves around your maypole, throwing them up into the air and letting them fall as they may, tossed by a breeze of your own making. Choose several ribbons with intention, with each representing an aspect of yourself you wish to integrate with the others. You might choose green for growth and renewal, red for passion and vitality, yellow for joy and creativity, blue for peace and inner wisdom, and purple for a connection to the mysteries of nature and its power. Join them together at the top of the maypole, securing them in place.

When you're ready to weave your maypole, pause to ground and center yourself. Take a few deep breaths, allowing yourself to become present in the moment. Connect with the earth beneath you, visualizing roots extending from your feet, anchoring you. If you like, speak silently or aloud this invocation honoring the union of the Green Man and the May Queen:

> *Green Man, infuse me with your untamed spirit.*
> *Fill me with the magic of the wilderness.*
> *May Queen, bestow upon me your nurturing love.*
> *Ignite the creative fire within my being.*
> *In this union of masculine and feminine divine*
> *I seek balance and harmony, together intertwined.*

Holding the ends of each ribbon, begin to weave them around the pole. This is a physical act that binds the spiritual within—and it takes both labor and artistry. Be creative as you wind your ribbons together, as each aspect of yourself comes together in union and balance. Put on some music and dance freely as you work, letting your movements flow naturally and joyfully, sipping your Maiwein as desired. As you come to the end of each ribbon, let it go—there's no need to secure it in place. It will unwind a little, but each released ribbon will be held by its companions in turn, all of the many and varied threads of your nature woven together into a harmonious whole.

And now, let the wild festivities begin! Uproot your maypole, dusting it off as need be, and place it on a table or hang it somewhere central, where you can see and appreciate it. Tuck any remaining flowers and leaves into the woven ribbons, celebrating the interwoven energies you carry within you. If it's safe to do so, light a bonfire, and pour libations of milk and Maiwein into its coals, giving thanks for nature's bounty and making sure to feel its presence in your life and enjoying all that it has to offer.

Week Twenty-Five

MAY MOON

May is the Flower Moon, which represents an abundant bursting forth of all that has been growing over the past several months. All that you have been planting and tending is ready to blossom—and now it is time for you to use that growth to manifest the next harvest that is yet to come.

Suggested Spell

Collect some brightly colored fresh or dried flowers like marigolds, roses, hibiscus, or lavender—whichever are accessible and meaningful to you. Remove the petals, setting the stems and leaves aside. Add the petals to a glass jar. Cover the petals with vodka or rubbing alcohol and let your potion sit for three days, surrounded by aventurine for growth and rose quartz for loving energy. Strain out the petals at the end of the third day.

Take a sheet of watercolor paper and a brush, and use the flower pigment to draw or write out what you wish to manifest this month, whether it's something open-ended like joy or abundance, or something more specific to you and your own life. Note that this painting will eventually fade, its color disappearing over time. This doesn't mean the spell is no longer in effect; in fact, it's simply been released into the air to do its work.

Week Twenty-Six

NEW MOON IN TAURUS

The new moon is Taurus is a time of great potential . . . but whatever is to come is not quite here yet. We remain in a liminal space, in which we have put in the hard work that Taurus requires but the results have not yet come to light. This is not an easy place to be! But it's also important to embrace this pause after so much doing and to allow whatever comes next to unfold.

Suggested Spell

On the night of the new moon, brew yourself a cup of calming tea to give you the patience you need to make it through this time. You'll need a combined total of a teaspoon's worth of the following dried herbs:

* **Chamomile, for calm**

* **Lavender, for peace**

* **Lemon balm, for an inner smile**

Blend them together in a mortar and pestle, putting any anxiety or nervous energy into this work. When you're ready, add herbs to a tea strainer and pour a cup of just-boiled water over them. As you allow your tea to steep, covered, for five to ten minutes, pull out your journal and write out anything you've been carrying, anything that you don't need to bring with you into this next lunar cycle. When your tea is ready, stir in honey and milk if you'd like, and then sip it as you cross out everything you've written—it's gone, over and done with.

Week Twenty-Seven

SUN IN GEMINI

When the sun is in Gemini, we are able to take advantage of Gemini's powers of clear communication, curiosity, versatility, and the ability to contain multitudes. We are able to stand in the light fully as we are, in all our many facets, and to speak our truths as well as hear the truth behind what others have to say.

Suggested Spell

Gather the following items:

- **A white feather, symbolic of the element of air, which rules over Gemini**

- **Clear quartz, for clarity and amplification**

- **A small bell or wind chime, to invoke air through sound**

Step outdoors and into the sunlight, if possible. Breathe in the fresh air while you hold the feather in your nondominant hand, allowing your thoughts to drift. Place the feather near you (being careful that it doesn't blow away in the breeze) and use the crystal to sound the bell or wind chime—it doesn't have to be loud, as you are the only one who needs to hear it. Consider what you have to say, and what you might have been holding back.

Inhale and exhale with sound, like blowing out a birthday candle, letting your breath join with the air around you. Let yourself be heard.

Wave the feather over the crystal, letting its energy infuse the clear quartz with the truth that air carries. Keep both the feather and crystal nearby, perhaps on your altar, to remind you of your own inner truth.

Week Twenty-Eight

FULL MOON IN SCORPIO

Scorpio is both intense and transformative, and when the light of the full moon shines upon that kind of energy, we can all experience heightened powers of intuition and psychic ability. We might see that which has been hidden from us, either by our own fears or a disguise created by societal expectations. Better still, we can also see deeply into ourselves, into our own shadows, helping us to know who we are and all that we could possibly choose to be.

Suggested Spell

On the night of the full moon, brew a batch of moon water to enhance self-reflection and help you gain clarity on what you see within. You'll need the following:

* **A clear glass or jar**

* **Clear quartz, for amplification and clarity**

* **Amethyst, for intuition and psychic ability**

Fill your glass with distilled water, and place it so that it sits beneath the light of the moon. Using your nondominant hand and holding each crystal in turn, focus your intentions for insight and clarity. Visualize the moonlight infusing the crystal with its pure and illuminating energy. Gently place the crystals into the water, allowing them to fall to the bottom of the glass. Allow the water to bask in the moonlight for the entire night, absorbing its energy.

In the morning, sip your moon water, taking its power into your body, nourishing yourself with it. You can also anoint your third eye or use the water for any other rituals you have in mind.

LITHA

June 21

THE SUMMER SOLSTICE IS THE LONGEST DAY OF THE year. For the Northern Hemisphere it is the day on which the North Pole is tilted closest to the sun. In the lands to the far north, that day can be almost unending, with the sun shining above the horizon even at the dead of night. The light of the midsummer sun brings vibrancy to the dappling leaves and energy to the buzzing insects and singing birds.

The Oak King is at the height of his powers on Litha, stronger than he has been before and stronger than he will be from this day forward. Once this longest day has ended, his powers will begin to wane, as the Holly King begins to grow in strength.

There are, of course, a variety of sun gods who shine brightest on Litha. A few to keep in mind are:

KĀNE, the Hawaiian creation god, who is linked to the concept of māna, or life energy, which flows through all living things. Kāne is the masculine god of fertility, fresh water, and the sun, and on Ke Alanui Polohiwa a Kāne, his life-giving energy is at its most potent.

AMATERASU, the Shinto goddess of the sun, who retreated into a cave because of the havoc caused by her brother Susanoo, the

impetuous god of storms—but as she hid, she plunged the world into darkness. Her siblings lured her out by placing a mirror at the entrance of the cave, enticing her with her own reflection and with the wildness of their dancing.

SOL, the Norse goddess of the sun, who drives a chariot across the sky, much like Apollo and Helios do in the warmer regions of Greece and Rome. Sol's brother Mani drives the moon, and together they traverse the heavens.

INTI, the Incan god of the sun, whose celebration of Inti Raymi took place over several days surrounding the solstice—Inti provided warmth and light, sustaining all life on earth.

You'll note that these deities vary in gender; so often these days we think of solar energy as masculine, but that wasn't always the case. It may be more useful to think of the sun as providing *growing* energy, a pulling upward from the earth. In her book *Wild Wisdom Companion*, Maia Toll describes the time of the summer solstice as the apex of light, as "the energy of thriving reaches a crescendo." The seeds sprout and the trees and plants grow during the waxing power of the Oak King—and they are not alone. We also push ourselves to grow, to stretch upward, seeking and striving.

The sun is the epitome of fire, and when it shines so brightly and for so long, it sparks something within us. Ever since the winter solstice, we have been growing and stretching, working toward manifesting all that we desire. Tomorrow, we will begin to recede and rest—but today, on this longest day, we are hovering in that moment of ultimate growth.

What will you do with all that fire? Like the ancients, will you pledge your troth to someone in the Litha tradition of handfasting that has grown into today's preference for a June wedding? Will you light a bonfire and keep it burning all night—however short that night may be—feeding the sun's power as long as you can? Will you scatter sage over the flames, calling upon its wisdom to bring illumination to all that remains unseen?

Or will you rest in this held breath of a day, standing as if on the peak of a mountain and surveying all that you have climbed, with the knowledge that it will be easier on the journey back down?

LITHA RITUAL TO EMBRACE THE POWER OF THE SUN

Wake up with the dawn. If you can, go out to witness the sun's rise, watching the darkness fade with the gentle dispersal of light. Sit and meditate for a few minutes, allowing the sun's energy to ease you into the day.

When it's time to get moving and begin your day, whether that means going to work or school, getting your household out the door, or sitting through traffic, hold on to those moments of peace and sit or stand a little straighter, stretching yourself up to the sun while letting it warm and energize you.

If you are able, step outside again at solar noon and lift your face to the sun. Briefly open your eyes, just long enough for the sun to imprint its image—don't damage your eyesight! Close them again, and watch as your eyes' memory of the sun shifts and changes, brighter even than the brightness of the sun behind your eyelids. Bring your feet together and find Samasthiti, or equal parts standing—grounding the base of the big toe, the base of the little toe, the inner corner of the heel, and the outer corner of the heel to come into balance. Stand up straight and tall, warm in the sun's fiery light. Feel your own sturdiness, and know that all of your growth comes from this place of strength within. Take that sense of balance and confidence with you as you continue your day.

At sunset, go out once more. If it's possible to find a place where you can watch the sun slide down into the horizon, do so—you'll learn that it's almost impossible to catch or predict that final moment, as if the sun is stretching out, holding on for just a little longer. When it does at last set, exhale a breath of gratitude for its warmth and light, shining for so long on the solstice—knowing, too, that it is still shining somewhere, and that it will, as always, return tomorrow.

If it's possible to work the following ritual at one of your pauses at sunrise, noon, or sunset, then do so, but it can be performed at any time during the solstice, even after the sun has gone down. Gather the following items:

* **A yellow candle and lighter or matches**

* **A glass jar with a lid**

* **Flowers that symbolize the sun, including sunflowers, daisies, marigolds, gladiolas, and black-eyed Susans—you'll want enough to fill the jar to the top**

* **An acorn**

* **An oak leaf**

* **Glue (optional)**

Use these materials to create an altar, surrounding the candle with flowers and setting the acorn and oak leaf aside. Sit or stand before your altar, finding that sense of powerful balance and feeling the line that stretches between you and the sun. When you light the candle, speak the following incantation:

> *I call upon the power of the sun and the spirit of the Oak.*
> *Fill me with your strength, your growth,*
> *your transformation.*

Working with one flower at a time, place them in your glass jar, laying each blossom with intentions for strength, confidence, light, and growth. With each flower, carefully pour in a little melted wax from your candle, sealing in its powers. Continue to layer the flowers and wax together, one by one, until the jar is full. Seal it closed.

Drip a last layer of wax atop the lid, then press the oak leaf into the hot wax before it dries. Drip a little more to then secure the acorn in place—don't worry if it doesn't really want to stay, as that simply means that physics is working. The intention remains, but if you like, you can add a dab of glue to make sure it sticks.

Keep your spell jar where you can see it. Watch as the flowers decay as the days grow shorter and the nights grow longer, remembering that this is a part of life and that it, too, leads to growth. Follow their example and begin to allow yourself to contemplate how you will find rest in the coming days, even as you bask in the energy and warmth you have gathered into yourself.

Week Twenty-Nine

JUNE MOON

Known as the Strawberry Moon or the Birth Moon, June's moon is the time when all that has been growing within us springs forth, ripe and golden with potential. Strawberries are associated with love, creativity, abundance, and vitality, as well as joy and celebration.

Suggested Spell

Buy a carton of fresh strawberries, from a farm stand if possible. If you can visit a pick-your-own farm, that's even better! Select the largest strawberry of the batch, then slice off the tip to create a flat surface. Using a small paring knife, carefully carve out a hollow in the center of the stem side, then place a small tea light inside it. As the candle burns, the sweet scent of strawberries will radiate positivity and joy. Thinly slice some multiple of three of the remaining strawberries and place them in a pitcher of water, allowing them to rest there for a few hours. As you drink the strawberry infusion, internalize their joy, vitality, and positive energy.

Week Thirty

NEW MOON IN GEMINI

The new moon in Gemini offers an opportunity to examine your connections with others. Although it can, this doesn't necessarily refer to your closest relationships, like these with romantic partners, family, or dear friends—instead, it's a good time to look at your wider social and professional circle. Gemini, with its strong communication and social skills, is valuable for networking—what kinds of connections do you want to manifest under its influence?

Suggested Spell

On the night of the new moon, write out a list of people in your life you'd like to be closer to, focusing not just on how they might improve your life in some way or other, but on whether or not you are drawn to them on a deeper level. Take a handful of pebbles and cast them onto a small cloth, then count how many stayed on the cloth. Moving down your list, count names until you reach the number of pebbles. (You may need to cycle through the list more than once.) Cross that name out. Repeat until only one name remains, and use this as a sign to reach out to that person in friendship and connection.

Week Thirty-One

SUN IN CANCER

When the warmth of the sun shines upon nurturing Cancer, we all have an opportunity for self-care. You may not feel like you need it right now—this is typically a time when things are going relatively well—but that is all the more reason to celebrate yourself! In fact, it can be easier to access and embrace self-love in these times, and then have a practice that you can carry with you when, inevitably, the more challenging times arise.

Suggested Spell

Create a blend of self-love bath salts by combining 3 cups of Epsom salts, ¼ cup of dried rose petals, ¼ cup of dried chamomile, and ¼ cup of dried lavender. Add 10 drops of rose essential oil, 10 drops of chamomile essential oil, and 10 drops of lavender essential oil, before mixing in ¼ cup of jojoba oil. If you're able to immerse your entire body in a bath, add all of the mixture to the bathwater, but if not, add a quarter cup of the mixture to a footbath. Light some candles, place some rose quartz nearby, and allow yourself to relax in the gentle warmth, letting any toxins or toxic thoughts leach into the water and drain away.

Week Thirty-Two

FULL MOON IN SAGITTARIUS

Sagittarius is a naturally adventurous and independent sign, eager to explore the world and all it has to offer. When that energy is touched by the creativity of the full moon, we can all experience that same desire for freedom and discovery. This week, let your curiosity guide you, and step outside of your routine. Take up more space—be *big* in yourself, and see where that takes you.

Suggested Spell

Gather an item or token that represents freedom to you. It might be a feather or a picture of a bird or it might be something that reminds you of a time when you were uninhibited and self-confident, like a playbill from a school play or something you created that you feel proud of. Place a candle so that its light shines upon your token, then take a small mirror and hold it, adjusting it until the light from the candle shines in your eyes, bouncing off of the token and back to you. Take it in, remembering that sense of courage and accomplishment, and then slide the token to the side. Take a sheet of paper and write down something new that you want to explore, letting the power of the flame spark within you.

Week Thirty-Three

JULY MOON

The Buck Moon of July is named for the male deer that have just begun sprouting their antlers. It is also known as the Thunder Moon for the summer storms that begin to blow across the land. Although the sun sets earlier these days, masculine/growing energy still abounds. How will you choose to take advantage?

Suggested Spell

Depending on where you live, the chances of a thunderstorm occurring this week are fairly low, but if one does, take advantage of it by collecting any rain that falls and saving this wildest of waters. Otherwise, go out in search of wild water that has not been harnessed by humans in any way. Find a stream, a pond, or the ocean—even a puddle will do! Place your water in a glass jar and add a tigereye crystal. Let it rest for a full day and night, until the crystal has been infused with the water's energy. Carry it with you whenever you need to be reminded of the wildness within you.

Week Thirty-Four

NEW MOON IN CANCER

This week Cancer's luminary is hidden from view. The moon is always there, of course, but the sun is not shining on it at present, and therefore its reflected light remains dark. How will you embrace this darkness? How will you care for yourself in all of your vulnerability?

Suggested Spell

Gather some grounding crystals like smoky quartz, obsidian, and black tourmaline—it is no coincidence that these crystals for protection are dark in color. There is safety in darkness, after all. On the night of the new moon, stand at the entrance to your home, opening your door and allowing the energy of the outside world to enter. Hold your chosen crystal in your nondominant hand, pressing it to your heart and letting it ground you. Close your door, and place the crystal on the floor,

sealing out the world. Repeat with any other entrances to your home, as well as your windows if you desire, leaving the crystals in place until morning.

Week Thirty-Five

SUN IN LEO

Whenever a sun appears in a certain sign, that sign's energy multiplies tenfold. But the sun is also Leo's luminary, and so Leo—already a little extra—becomes a powerhouse. This kind of energy may feel a little intimidating, but if you are willing, Leo's charisma, creativity, and generosity can help you step into the sun.

Suggested Spell

Use the power of the sun to create a sigil using light-sensitive paper available at most craft stores or online. First, write out what you want to manifest with Leo's powerful energy. Perhaps it might be something simple, like *I Am Powerful* or *I Am Creative*, or you might have something more specific in mind. Once you've decided on your phrase, eliminate all but the first letter of each word, as well as any repeated letters. Take a pencil and sketch out a very simple design using these letters—ordinarily, we want to make our sigils fairly elaborate to obscure the meaning and give them power, but in this case the sun will do that for us. Use a pair of scissors to carefully cut out the outline of this design. Position it on your solar paper, then place the paper in the light of the sun, letting it rest there for several minutes. When the paper has transformed from light to dark blue, remove your cutout and rinse the paper in cool water, fixing your sigil in place.

Week Thirty-Six

FULL MOON IN CAPRICORN

At first glance, Capricorn doesn't seem to match well with lunar energy. As an earth sign, Capricorn is grounded and practical, ambitious and hardworking, but not typically prone to the flights of imagination and mystery we think of when contemplating the full moon. However, Capricorn is also skilled at strategy and manifestation, both of which work very well with moonlight's power.

Suggested Spell

On the night of the full moon, create a manifestation anointing oil. Gather the following ingredients:

* **Frankincense essential oil, to gather your energy**

* **Mint essential oil, for clarity and focus**

* **Orange essential oil, for positivity**

* **Patchouli essential oil, for abundance and self-confidence**

Mix nine drops of each with two tablespoons of a soothing carrier oil, like sweet almond or jojoba. Place the mixture in a small bowl, surrounding it with the following crystals:

* **Citrine, for abundance**

* **Green aventurine, for luck and opportunity**

* **Moonstone, to harness the moon's energy**

* **Pyrite, for confidence and willpower**

Let it rest in the light of the full moon while you breathe and meditate for several minutes, envisioning all that you choose to manifest and allow in your life. When you're ready, use the oil to anoint the soles of your feet, your wrists, your heartspace, the base of your throat, and the top of your head.

LAMMAS

August 1

THE IMAGE WE HOLD IN MIND FOR LAMMAS IS ALWAYS the same—a sheaf of grain, freshly harvested and ready to be transmuted into life-sustaining bread. Peaches, blueberries, and grapes burst into life, coloring the landscape, and tomatoes split their skins as they ripen. The possibilities of the growing time of the year have reached their fruition . . . but that doesn't mean the work is done. We have sown all that we can, and now it is time to reap. The seeds that we have nurtured into full growth must now be cut down, as we take in what they have to offer, nurturing ourselves in turn.

Lammas falls on the midpoint between the summer solstice and the autumnal equinox, and as such it opens the door to autumn. August is by no means cool in terms of temperature—the hottest days of the year typically fall around Lammas—but it is the flush of a heat that is about to wane, in one last push before the enforced rest of winter.

Lammas is derived from the term *loaf-mass* and is often associated with the folk figure John Barleycorn. The subject of ballads and folk-tales dating back to the early Middle Ages, John Barleycorn, as a person-ification of the barley crop, embodies the spirit of the harvest.

They ploughed, they sowed, they harrowed him in
Threw clods upon his head
And they've sworn a solemn oath
John Barleycorn was dead.
Then they let him lie for a very long time,
Till the rain from heaven did fall;
Then little Sir John sprung up his head,
And soon amazed them all.
They let him stand till midsummer's day
Till he looked both pale and wan,
And little Sir John's grown a long, long beard,
And so become a man.

The ballad goes on to describe the trials endured by John Barleycorn, as he is cut down at the knees, bound to a cart, and ground between millstones. It's a surprisingly emotional way to look at the cycle of growth and harvest, acknowledging the sacrifices offered by the life-giving plants that sustain us. The interplay between mythology, folklore, and the seasonal cycles of agricultural practices serves as a reminder of the cycles of life and death, the bounty of the earth, and the importance of gratitude for the sustenance provided by the harvest.

But John Barleycorn is not the only folkloric figure with connections to this first harvest, for Lammas is also known as Lughnasadh. Lugh is the Celtic sun god, and he fought battle after battle before finally defeating Balor, who had covered the land in darkness and drought. But the fields of Ireland were then sodden with blood, and nothing would grow. And so Lugh's mother Tailtiu gave her body to clear the fields for agriculture, healing the land. Lugh held a festival in her honor on the day of the first harvest, a tradition which has held to this day.

Whether we call it Lammas or Lughnasadh, this is a day of celebration but also of mourning, of gratitude for the sacrifices made so that we can live. In our modern age, most of us live at a distance from agriculture—we do not sow and neither do we reap. But a pint of beer at the local pub and a croissant from a favorite bakery have their roots in the same cycle of growth, offering, and decay. On this day, honor the work and sacrifice that go into the luxuries we may take for granted. If you're able, walk in a field, feeling the press of the earth beneath your feet. Visit a farm stand and taste the newly harvested fruits and vegetables, the terroir of the earth that grew them giving them a flavor that is tied to place and the soil that lies beneath us.

LAMMAS RITUAL TO HONOR THE EARTH

When you go to a farm stand, whether it's on the side of the road or at a farmers market, gather enough for a feast. Follow the guidance of your eyes—if you're drawn to brightly colored fruits—and to your sense of smell—if you're drawn to the sharp, green scents of vegetables and herbs. Frequently you'll be able to find some stalks of wheat or barley, often for sale as decoration, but if not, purchase some fresh corn. If you like, buy some beer, as well.

Spend your day preparing for your feast, inviting any chosen friends or family to share in the celebration with you. Start by baking a loaf of bread—it is loaf-mass, after all.

In a large mixing bowl, combine 4 cups of bread flour and 1 teaspoon of salt. Stir with a wooden spoon, incorporating the grains of salt. Sprinkle with just a tiny bit of dried herbs, including thyme for vitality, rosemary for remembrance, and calendula for abundance.

In a separate, smaller bowl, pour 1½ cups of warm water. Stir in a tablespoon of honey for its sweet abundance, then sprinkle in 2 teaspoons of active dry yeast. Breathe into it, letting your breath awaken the yeast, then let the mixture sit for five minutes while the yeast sparks to life.

Make a well in the flour and herbs, then pour in the yeast mixture. Stir with a wooden spoon, incorporating the two into one craggy mass. Transfer the dough onto a clean, lightly floured surface. Knead the dough for five to ten minutes, putting some gentle force into it. You might imagine John Barleycorn, beaten and ground down, or Tailtiu tilling the soil with her lifeblood. Do this work in their honor.

Shape the dough into a ball and place it in an oiled bowl. Cover it with a dishcloth and let it rise for about one to two hours, surrounded with carnelian for abundance, sunstone for vitality, and tigereye for personal power. Wait until the dough has doubled in size, growing so that it may transform.

Preheat your oven to 400 degrees, and place a baking sheet or dish inside. Once the dough has fully risen, punch it down gently, then turn it out onto the floured surface, shaping it into a loaf. As you do so, work in your intentions and your gratitude. Gently place the loaf onto the preheated baking dish, then bake for around thirty to forty minutes, or until the bread is golden brown and sounds hollow when you tap on its crust.

Continue with the remaining preparations for your feast, but make sure to set aside a quiet moment for a brief ritual. Make a corn or grain dolly by shucking an ear of corn or using the stalks of grain, if they were available at the market. Soak them in water for thirty minutes or until they are pliable, then bend your grain in half, making a loop at the top. Bind it in place with string or yarn, so that the seed heads or the ends of the cornstalks form the body. You can decide how you want to decorate your dolly, making it masculine in honor of John Barleycorn or feminine in honor of Tailtiu—or somewhere in between.

Hold the dolly in your hand, and speak the following invocation:

John Barleycorn, the spirit of the grain,
Through your sacrifice and rebirth, you rise again.
As the golden fields sway in the summer breeze,
I honor your presence and blessings you release.
Tailtiu, mother of the land, provider of life,
Your strength and devotion labored after toil and strife.
You nurtured the soil with love and care
For the abundant harvest we now share.

Pour a small offering of beer or water into a bowl or chalice, and sprinkle in the following:

* **Flour, for nourishment, transformation, and community**

* **Salt, for cleansing, protection, and longevity**

* **Sugar, for vitality, celebration, and love**

Take a sip, bringing these blessings into your body with gratitude for all they offer. Then return them to the earth, pouring the remainder into the soil outside or into a potted plant.

When it is time for the celebrations to begin, open the feasting by breaking off a piece of bread and passing the loaf around so that everyone present can take a share. Consume it thoughtfully and with intention. If you like, you can speak aloud any gratitudes or intentions you may have on this day and offer space for everyone else to do the same. Hold a moment of silence and reverence for all that the world has to offer, as well as for all that you have each worked to grow over the course of these many months. And then, allow the celebrations to begin, sharing food and beer in laughter and joy.

Week Thirty-Seven

AUGUST MOON

August's moon is known as the Sturgeon Moon for the fish of the Great Lakes, which are said to be more easily caught beneath its light. But it is also referred to by the Cree people as the Flying Up Moon, named for when young birds are finally ready to leave their nests. We, too, are ready to leave the nests we've been so steadily building for ourselves over the course of these many moons, ready to explore the world, knowing that we have a foundation to return to whenever we need it.

Suggested Spell

Use this week to work on your altar—if you don't already have one, it's time to create one! For the August moon, you'll want to incorporate the element of air, adding feathers, a bell, and images that remind you of air, like the King of Swords from a tarot deck or a picture of birds in flight. You might even place an athame, or ritual knife, there—it doesn't need to be sharp, as it's simply a *symbol* of your ability to cut through all that has been tying you down. The element of air will make your altar a place where you can find the truth, and as you meditate in front of it, your inner eye will see all the more clearly.

Week Thirty-Eight

NEW MOON IN LEO

The new moon gives fiery Leo energy a moment to cool off and take stock. Instead of rushing about to your next task or creative project, you have an opportunity to sit with what's going on internally, searching inside yourself for what will truly light you up when the moon begins to wax in the days to come.

Suggested Spell

Choose a candle, and anoint it with an essential oil that aligns well with the energy of Leo, like frankincense, myrrh, orange, cinnamon, or rose—whichever appeals to you the most. Light the candle in a dimly lit room, and watch the smoke begin to curl. Smoke-scrying is an intuitive art, so as you notice how it swirls, twist, or billows, remain open to any impressions, insights, or messages that come to you. If you like, do a little artistic journaling, echoing the swirls of smoke with your pen or pencil, forming them into words that inspire you. What will you bring forth in this new lunar cycle?

Week Thirty-Nine

SUN IN VIRGO

Meticulous Virgo shines brightly at this time, with an energy of practicality, efficiency, and analytical thinking that counters the impulsive energy of Leo we are now leaving behind. You can use the grounded skills of Virgo to perfect the experimental creativity you've been enjoying recently—you might do a little research this week or perhaps revise a project you've been working on.

Suggested Spell

Practice a grounding meditation by lying flat on the earth, outdoors, and if possible, beneath the shade of a tree. Watch the leaves move against the light above you, and notice how when you close your eyes you can still see that light flickering. Feel the weight of your body against the earth, and visualize the earth rising beneath you, holding you up. Let any restlessness drain out of you, leaching into the soil below. Fill the space this creates with the gentle, loving support of the earth, so that you can carry it with you, knowing you have a firm foundation within.

Week Forty

FULL MOON IN AQUARIUS

Aquarius is a curious and independent sign, but for all its autonomy, Aquarius is also deeply invested in the good of humanity as a whole. Social consciousness comes to light beneath this full moon, and you may feel the importance of a sense of community, even as you value your own freedom. The two needs are not in opposition to each other, for sometimes it is only in the company of those who see us as we are that we feel most truly ourselves.

Suggested Spell

Use the energy of Aquarius's moon to do some good in your community. Choose a cause that has meaning for you personally, something that sparks your interest as well as your commitment. Working for

social justice is unfortunately often a little discouraging—the more we learn about injustice, the more we feel inadequate in our attempts to make things better. But you *do* have the power to make a difference. Remind yourself of this by casting an empowerment spell with a pentagram, a traditional symbol of strength and power. You'll need a piece of paper, a pen, and five small objects—coins, small stones, etc. Draw a pentagram, and place an object at each of the points, setting an intention for each object:

SELF-CONFIDENCE: you have the power to create change

PERSONAL GROWTH: you are always evolving and learning

INNER STRENGTH: you have the resources to do difficult things

SELF-LOVE: do not neglect your own needs while serving others

AUTHENTICITY: trust yourself to know what is right and just

MABON

September 21

MABON OCCURS ON THE AUTUMNAL EQUINOX WHEN, once again, day is equal to night. It is a threshold, the moment after which the nights will be longer than the days. It is on this night that the Holly King and the Oak King come together once more in battle—but this time, it is the Holly King who is victorious, and the Oak King's power no longer holds sway.

Unlike the other pagan holidays, Mabon's name has no basis in history. The celebration itself dates back thousands of years in varying forms and under various folkloric aegises, but the term applied to it is only fifty years old. During the Wiccan resurgence of the 1970s, poet and academic Aidan Kelly gave the holiday the name of the Welsh god Mabon.

Mabon ap Modron was the son of the Great Mother goddess, but his birth remains something of a mystery—his father is not named, though some mythologists believe him to have been Amaethon, the god of agriculture. Whoever sired him, Mabon was taken from Modron when he was only three nights old—and again, it is never stated who abducted him. Whoever they were, they imprisoned him in Caer Loyw, which translates to the "House of Steel." And there he remained, forgotten by the world.

Until one day, he was rescued by Culhwch (pronounced KUHL-hwuk), a hero figure of Welsh tales. Culhwch was in love with the maiden Olwen, but her father, the villainous giant Ysbaddaden Bencawr, did not believe he was worthy. And so, following the pattern of many a folktale, Ysbaddaden set Culhwch a series of impossible tasks.

Culhwch sought assistance from a variety of figures, including King Arthur, in order to complete one of his many tasks: to kill the mystical boar Twrch Trwyth. (Welsh names make for a fun challenge, and this one is pronounced TOORKH THROO-ith.) The Great Boar was said to be nearly impossible to track, but despite his isolation and captivity, Mabon was known to possess untold secrets. And so Culhwch found and freed him, and in return Mabon used his unique abilities to navigate and interpret celestial signs and omens, allowing him to pinpoint the location of Twrch Trwyth. Mabon continued to follow Culhwch on his quest, using his strength and agility to retrieve magical items as needed, battle adversaries, and so forth, until at last Culhwch returned to Ysbaddaden victorious and married Olwen as promised.

And that is the end of Mabon's story, as he is merely a side character. He's not the hero of the tale; he's simply one of the merry band who accompanies Culhwch. We may well wonder whether Mabon was actually all that merry, having been imprisoned for his entire life—but on the other hand, maybe he was filled with scampering joy at his newfound freedom. The stories do not say.

There are a lot of unknowns in Mabon's story, and perhaps it is for those reasons that Kelly's choice for this fairly mysterious holiday has managed to live on. Kelly wanted a figure that fit the "underworld prisoner" trope, as an echo of Persephone's return to Hades, which occurs on the autumnal equinox. Mabon is a figure of rebirth, renewal, and the recovery of lost knowledge. He, like so many other mythical figures, represents the eternal cycle of life, and his rescue symbolizes the restoration of balance and harmony to the world.

And yet, the autumnal equinox, a time of balance when day is equal to night, is not a doorway into the light, but rather into the darkness. On this night, we enter the realm of the Holly King. All the growing and striving and work we've done since Ostara can finally be laid to rest. Mabon stands as the final harvest, the point at which we must survey what we have gathered and determine whether it will be enough to see us through the long winter night—and yet, if it is not, we will have to make do, for the night is here and nothing will stave it off.

That feels a bit ominous, for there is mystery and uncertainty in the darkness. Mabon himself was full of uncertainty and received no answers—who his father was, who imprisoned him: he would never know. But he did somehow hold other knowledge—precious and secret perceptions and skills that could be used to guide others to find their own answers. He is a tragic figure, but also an inspirational one, for he recovered from his time in darkness and went on to live a life of adventure in service to one of the great heroes of Wales.

Then again, perhaps there's another way to look at it. Perhaps it was his time in darkness and solitude that provided him with his precious, unique understanding. Perhaps the time of the Holly King may indeed feel like a kind of prison, when we are shut indoors, huddling away from the cold—but it is one that offers us the opportunity to learn from within.

Darkness is more than a place of fear and uncertainty—it also allows us to rest. When we sleep, our minds take stock, working through our dreams to understand and process our days. Our bodies heal, and our emotions find balance and peace. And in that space of rest and rejuvenation, our creativity can blossom and grow. The same word—*to dream*—is used for the experiences that occur when we sleep in the darkness and the aspirational wishes we can fulfill in the daylight. In the night, we dream and gain secret knowledge about ourselves—and about what might be possible in the world.

MABON RITUAL TO EMBRACE
THE DARKNESS

The ideal time to perform this ritual is right at sunset, the threshold over which we step into the night. Light a candle just as the sun goes down, and sit in this dim light—for it is still light out, the refracting rays of the sun shining even though the orb itself has dipped below the horizon. It is a darkness in which we can still see.

You'll need the following items:

* **A fresh apple**

* **A small knife or athame (sharp enough to cut)**

* **A pen**

* **A small piece of paper**

* **A handful of dried, crumbly leaves**

Hold the apple in your hands, feeling its shape. Note how the color of its skin shifts, as well as any flaws you can find. Inhale its scent. The apple is a symbol of hidden knowledge and wisdom—envision it as a vessel of secrets waiting to be shared.

Take your athame and carefully carve into the top of the apple, focusing your intent on unlocking this secret understanding. Hollow out the core and pull it out, leaving a hole in the center of the apple.

In the light of your candle, write out your intention, being specific about the kind of inner knowledge you seek. Fold the paper several times, until it is small enough to fit into the apple. Crumble your dead leaves over the paper, adding in the wisdom they hold, and then cover them with the stem of the apple, sealing it all in.

Cup the apple in your hands and speak the following invocation:

Mabon, holder of hidden wisdom,
I invoke your presence and guidance.
As I delve into the realms of secret knowledge
Guide me on this journey of understanding.

Hold the apple close to your heart as you look into the candle. Watch it flicker and move with the unseen wind of your own breath, of the mysterious flow of air that makes it dance. Let your eyes blur and your mind open, welcoming any insights, symbols, or messages that may arise during this quiet contemplation. Be receptive to any intuitive knowledge that may come to you.

When you're ready, consume the apple. You may want to use your athame to slice it to avoid accidentally ingesting any bits of leaves or paper—but don't worry, their energy has infused the apple with all you need.

Continue with your evening, celebrating the sabbat with family or friends as you choose, perhaps enjoying some mulled apple cider or stuffed pumpkins or even apple pie. When you're ready for sleep, take a few moments to center yourself, reflecting back on what you saw before and after eating the apple. Lie back in your bed in the darkness, and find that sense of openness again. As you dive down into the realm of sleep, imagine Mabon standing before you, newly freed from his imprisonment, holding knowledge that no one else has. Understand that you too carry secrets within you, and that your dreams can summon them from the depths. Let Mabon be your guide in the darkness.

When you wake, take a few moments just on the edge of sleep, recalling any dreams you may have had. Write them down. And then, as you go on with your day, consider ways in which you can use the knowledge you have gained. Follow your intuition as Mabon followed the stars, wherever it may lead you.

Week Forty-One

SEPTEMBER MOON

If the September full moon falls close to the autumnal equinox, it is the Harvest Moon—but that isn't always the case, as sometimes that full moon occurs in October in another example of the Gregorian calendar not quite matching up with the movements of the spheres. The Harvest Moon represents abundance and gratitude for all you have reaped—it is a conclusion, but also a new beginning. Just as Mabon is a threshold between light and darkness, the Harvest Moon is a liminal space . . . and there is power in that. It's a particularly potent time for spellwork and ritual, whether it falls in September or October.

The September Moon is otherwise the Corn Moon, which is symbolic of abundance as well as protection. Beneath the light of the Corn Moon, you can rest assured that you have all you need.

Suggested Spell

Create a corn candleholder for your altar. Take a dried corncob—the kind sold for decoration—and cut it so it has a flat base. Trim the other end, and then using a small, sharp knife, carefully hollow out the inside until you can fit in a tapered candle. Light the candle to invite corn's energy of safety and abundance into your life.

Week Forty-Two

NEW MOON IN VIRGO

With the potential and new beginnings offered by the new moon, it's a good idea to take advantage of Virgo's ability to analyze, organize, and plan. As you enter into a new phase, consider what you may want to manifest over the course of this lunar cycle. Use Virgo's practicality to figure out your next steps.

Suggested Spell

Do a little journaling, figuring out a practical, step-by-step plan for what you may want to focus on this week. Keep in mind that this doesn't need to mean *accomplishing* anything. You may want to manifest more time to rest, more self-care, the ability to finish a TV show uninterrupted—all of which are totally valid desires! Figure out what needs to happen to make this possible. Tear a paper into small pieces and write each step on an individual piece—it doesn't matter how many steps there are. Set them in a line on your altar, and cover each one with a crystal, choosing those that align with the energy of that step. For example, you might put moonstone on "go to bed earlier" or aquamarine, which is good for communication, on "request uninterrupted time." As you go through each step this week, tackling one at a time, carry that crystal in your pocket to support you.

Week Forty-Three

SUN IN LIBRA

Libra's ability to find balance and harmony in even the most challenging of situations is something to be cherished. Libra's ruling planet is Venus, and when combined with the energy of the new moon in Virgo, the kind of love she enables is sustainable—a love that fills you even as you give to others.

Suggested Spell

Gather two crystals that resonate with Libra's energy, choosing from the following list based on what you need in this moment:

* **Blue lace agate, for calm and clear communication**

* **Lepidolite, for emotional balance and harmony**

* **Rose quartz, for harmony, compassion, and unconditional love**

* **Selenite, for clarity and spiritual growth**

Cup a crystal in each hand, holding them lightly in your curled fingers. Stand firm and tall, grounding in your feet, then inhale as you stretch your arms out wide, pulling the crystals apart from each other and arching your back slightly to gaze up at the sky. Exhale and bring your hands back together at your chest, curling forward slightly, bending your head, bowing in service to your heart. Repeat this moving meditation for several breaths, feeling the love you have to offer the world, even as you hold it for yourself.

Week Forty-Four

FULL MOON IN PISCES

The full moon in Pisces is a magical time, as the creativity and flow of Pisces is lit up with the mystery and energy of the full moon. The merging of these two complementary forces makes for a powerful time, and you should consider what kind of magic you want to work on the night of this full moon, as your powers will be amplified.

Suggested Spell

The moon holds watery energy, as Pisces does as well, of course. A ritual bath can help prepare you for whatever guidance the moon will give on this night. You'll need the following items:

* **A handful of fresh or dried clary sage, to enhance psychic ability**

* **A handful of fresh or dried lavender, to relax the mind**

* **A handful of fresh or dried mugwort, to stimulate dreams, visions, and intuition**

* **A handful of fresh or dried rosemary, to clear the mind and heighten focus**

* **A mortar and pestle**

* **A large ceramic bowl**

Add your herbs to your mortar and pestle and bruise them, mixing them together and using the power of your hands and your strength to release their energy. Put them in your bowl, then sprinkle in three handfuls of water, stirring gently with your fingers. Add more water until the bowl is comfortably full but not overflowing. (You don't want to have to worry about spilling it.) Then place it where it can rest in the moonlight for several minutes. Go through your evening routine, preparing for bed, but just before you go to sleep, return to your moon water. Dip your fingers in and use the water to bathe your face, your temples, your wrists, and the base of your throat. You can use just the tips of your fingers if you want to avoid getting bits of herbs everywhere—the water holds all that you need. When you sleep, pay attention to any dreams that come to you, listening for what they have to tell you.

Week Forty-Five

OCTOBER MOON

If the full moon of October is not the Harvest Moon, it is the Hunter's Moon. Its light favors the seeker, guiding you toward whatever might be hidden. You see things more clearly beneath the Hunter's Moon, including other people's intentions toward you, the potential outcomes of certain situations, and, most importantly, your own gifts and passions.

Suggested Spell

Step into the light of the Hunter's Moon by crafting a truth serum. You'll need the following:

* **A handful of fresh sage, for wisdom**

* **Three bay leaves, fresh or dried, for uncovering hidden truths**

* **A handful of fresh mint, for clarity**

Bruise all the herbs in a mortar and pestle, working in your intentions for revealing what is hidden. Add them to a glass jar, cover them with a neutral unscented oil, and allow them to steep for the full lunar cycle. When the oil is ready, use it to anoint your third eye right between your brows so that you can perceive the truth.

Week Forty-Six

NEW MOON IN LIBRA

Libra's new moon is an opportunity to work on new relationships—these can be romantic relationships or friendships or even a new way of perceiving a relationship that has been in existence for some time. When something is new, you have the ability to set the pattern for how you want it to be going forward—Libra offers the example of balance, maintaining a harmony between your needs and the needs of the other person.

Suggested Spell

Set some intentions for what you would like to see in this relationship, whether it's laughter, connection, communication, or even something more specific like "texting each other while watching our favorite shows." Gather a handful of stackable rocks—rivers are a great place to do this, as are some beaches. Stack your rocks one on top of the other, assigning a specific intention to each one. If they fall, adjust—finding balance is what this is about, and you may discover that some rocks need to be set aside in favor of others. Learn from them what they tell you.

Week Forty-Seven

SUN IN SCORPIO

Scorpio has an intense energy that is often focused inward, but when it is brought into the light of the sun, that energy can be fixed on the outside world—and not just the everyday world, but the hidden, mystical realm of the things we know to be true even if we can't explain them. Scorpio longs to understand—even that which cannot truly be grasped in any logical way.

Suggested Spell

Embrace that dichotomy by working to understand with your heart, rather than your mind. You'll need the following:

* **A green or pink candle, whichever color most resonates for you with heart-focused energy, and lighter or matches**

* **Rose quartz or green aventurine crystal**

Find a quiet place for reflection, then light your candle, placing the crystal beside it. As you do so, visualize the warm and gentle light filling the space around you with love and compassion. Cup the crystal in your hand and hold it to your heart. Imagine your heart opening, allowing the information brought to light by the candle to fill you, giving you the kind of understanding that has no name, but is true nonetheless. Listen to your heart's wisdom.

Week Forty-Eight

FULL MOON IN ARIES

When the fiery power of Aries meets the watery energy of the moon, you may feel a little unsettled—emotions run high, your desires feel stronger than ever, and you may have a brighter picture of your own identity in all its complexity. This kind of turbulence is a *good* thing, even if it can be a little uncomfortable. See where it takes you.

Suggested Spell

Fire and water are opposites, but we all contain multitudes. This spell will help you embrace your own contradictory nature. You'll need a candle as well as a bowl of water—when you light the candle, stare into its flame and recognize the ways in which it represents you. Are you unpredictable, creative, passionate? Then, look into the bowl of water, gazing at your reflection. What do you see there? Are you mutable, emotional, intuitive? Raise the candle and carefully allow some of the melted wax to drip into the water. Then, dip your fingers into the bowl and gently flick small drops at the flame. They may be opposites, but they can coexist, just as your dualities can come together within you.

Conclusion

WHAT HAPPENS NOW?

At the end of a year of practice in finding magic in the everyday and seeking to honor the wheel of the year . . . what has changed?

In some ways, very little. There are still groceries to buy and dishes to do. There are still irritants and anxieties and practicalities to manage—and the never-ending struggle to balance our own needs with the needs of those around us. These are the basic components of our lives, and they aren't going anywhere.

And yet *everything* has changed. Because now we are practiced in how to view those struggles with intention and with the knowledge that we have resources within ourselves and the natural world around us to transform those struggles into something meaningful and magical. We can stand in line at the grocery store behind the woman who is seemingly buying one of everything and find a moment of quiet within. We can remind ourselves that each lunar cycle and each astrological shift is a guide to how we can hold ourselves and those around us with compassion. We can find balance, passion, creativity, inspiration, and joy in even the smallest, seemingly most mundane things because we now know that they can hold the most meaning. Like flowers growing in the cracks of concrete, the inspiration that bursts from the unremarkable is all the more beautiful and magical.

You hold the power to create magic in the everyday. By embracing your inner power, trusting your intuition, and cultivating a deep connection with the natural world, you have found the living, breathing energy that flows through every moment of your existence. Welcome it with open arms, nurture it, and you will continue to live a life filled with magic ... throughout the wheel of the year.

Acknowledgments

Basically, I have to thank my editor, Shannon Fabricant. We've been on quite a journey together, and every time I think, "This is probably the last one. She's got to be tired of me by now." And then she says, "What do you think about this?" I'll admit, at first I'm always hesitant, thinking I can't possibly have anything left to say . . . and then I always find something new and interesting and, whoops, turns out I have *lots* to say.

I know perfectly well how fortunate I am, and how much of a book's success relies on just about everyone except the author (in my case, anyway). In addition to Shannon, Kristin Kiser, Susan Van Horn, Amber Morris, Ashley Benning, Amy Cianfrone, Kara Thornton, Ana-Maria Bonner, Elizabeth Parks, Annie Brag, Betsey Hulsebosch—you are the ones who make this happen, and I'm so honored and grateful.

Neil, you really went above and beyond with this one, and your feedback and research are not only helpful, but inspiring. You make life so magical. John Barleycorn's got your back. Dave, thanks for keeping the porch interruptions to a minimum and always providing tea and coffee as needed. Ellie and Hardy, thanks for your company.

Index

agate, 31

ajna. See third eye chakra *(ajna)*

All Souls' Day, 1

Amaethon, 109

Amaterasu, 81-82

amber, 13

amethyst, 8, 13, 31, 42, 57, 78

ancestors, Samhain and, 5-6, 7

ancestral altar, 7-8

anger, releasing, 61-63

Aphrodite, 67

April moon (week twenty-one), 60-61

aquamarine, 116

Aquarius

    full moon in (week forty), 105-106

    new moon in (week fourteen), 43-44

    sun in (week eleven), 30-32

Aries

    full moon in (week forty-eight),
       123-124

    new moon in (week twenty-two),
       61-63

    sun in (week nineteen), 57-58

athame, 102-103, 112

August moon (week thirty-seven),
    102-103

autumnal equinox. *See* Mabon
    (September 21)

aventurine, 45, 73-74

azurite, 57

Baldr, 19

Balor, 98

Barleycorn, John, 97-98, 100-101

Beaver Moon (week one), 9-10

Beira, 1-2

Beltane (May 1), 67-72

    ritual to explore the wildness
       within, 69-72

besom, 38

bird/hare, 50, 51-52

Birth Moon, 86

black pepper essential oil, 11

black tourmaline, 27, 42, 91

bloodstone, 11, 22, 31

blue lace agate, 42, 117

blue topaz, 22

bonfires

    Beltane, 72

    Imbolc, 39-40

    Samhain, 1, 8

    Yule, 22

bread, baking, 99-100, 101

Breaking Ice Moon, 60

Brigid, 35-38

Brigid's cross, 38-39

Buck Moon, 91-92

Cailleach, 1-2, 8

Cancer

    full moon in (week twelve), 32-33

    new moon in (week thirty-four),
       91-92

    sun in (week thirty-one), 88-89

Capricorn

    full moon in (week thirty-six), 94-95

    new moon in (week ten), 29-30

carnelian, 31, 42

Cernunnos, 67

citrine, 13, 45, 95

cleansing bath, 45

clear quartz, 22, 42, 60, 76, 78

clootie wells, 37-38, 39

Cold Moon, 23-24

corn/grain dolly, 100-101

Corn Moon, 115

crone witches, 1-2

crows, 17

crystals. *See individual crystals*
Culhwch, 110
Cullen, Mary Teresa, 35

Dagda, 36
December moon, light of the (week five), 23-24
Deutsche Mythologie (Grimm), 49
Día de Muertos (Day of the Dead), 1, 5-6
Dionysus, 67
dreams/dreaming
  December moon and, 24
  full moon in Pisces and, 119
  holly and, 18
  Mabon and, 111, 113
  mugwort and, 119
  new moons and, 29
  sun in Pisces and, 44-45
  yew and, 20
"dumb supper," 5

eggs, coloring, 51-54
Eostre, 49-51, 53, 68
everyday, creating power of magic in, 127-128

fears, Samhain and buried, 3-4, 7
February moon (week thirteen), 41-42
Flora, 68
Flower Moon, 73
fluorite, 27, 57
Flying Up Moon, 102-103
Fomorians, 36
Freya, 49, 68
Frigga, 19
Frost Moon (week one), 9-10
full moon
  in Aquarius (week forty), 105-106
  in Aries (week forty-eight), 123-124
  in Cancer (week twelve), 32-33
  in Capricorn (week thirty-six), 94-95
  in Gemini (week eight), 26-27
  in Leo (week sixteen), 45-46
  in Libra (week twenty-four), 64-65
  in Pisces (week forty-four), 118-119
  in Sagittarius (week thirty-two), 89-90
  in Scorpio (week twenty-eight), 77-78
  in Taurus (week four), 14-15
  in Virgo (week twenty), 59-60

garnet, 31
Gemini
  full moon in (week eight), 26-27
  new moon of (week thirty), 87
  sun in (week twenty-seven), 75-77
Goibhniu, 36
green aventurine, 95, 123
Green Man, 67-69, 71
Grimm, Jacob, 49
grounding meditation, 105

Hades, 110
Halloween, 1
Hamlet, 20
handfasting, 82
hare, 50, 51-52
Harvest Moon, 114-115
hawthorn branch, for maypole or May Branch, 69-70
hawthorn tree (May Tree), 67
hieros gamos, 68-69
Hod, 19
holly, 18, 21, 31
Holly King, 18-21, 22, 81, 109, 111
howling at the moon, 28-29
Hunger Moon, 41-42
Hunter's Moon, 120-121

Imbolc (February 7), 35-40
  clootie wells, 37-38, 39
  ritual for growth and healing, 38-40

incantations
    February moon, 42
    Imbolc, 39-40
    Litha, 84
intentions
    Brigid's cross and, 38
    Hunter's Moon and, 121
    Lammas and, 100, 101
    Litha and, 84-85
    Mabon, 112-113
    new moon in Libra and, 122
    Ostara and, 54
    sun in Aquarius and, 31-32
    sun in Sagittarius and, 12-13
    Yule, 22
Inti, 82
invocations
    Lammas, 101
    Mabon, 113
    maypole, 71
    Ostara, 53

Jack-in-the-Green, 67
January moon (week nine), 28-29
journaling
    new moon in Leo and, 104
    new moon in Scorpio and, 11
    new moon in Taurus and, 75
    new moon in Virgo and, 116
    Samhain ritual and, 6-7
July moon (week thirty-three), 90-91
June moon (week twenty-nine), 86

Kāne, 81
keens, 36
Kelly, Aidan, 109, 110
Kildare Cathedral, 35-36
King Arthur, 110

labradorite, 57
Lammas (August 1), 97-101
    ritual to honor the earth, 99-101

lapis lazuli, 8, 31, 57
Leo
    full moon in (week sixteen), 45-46
    new moon in (week thirty-eight),
        103-104
    sun in (week thirty-five), 92-93
lepidolite, 117
Libra
    full moon in (week twenty-four),
        64-65
    new moon in (week forty-six), 121-122
    sun in (week forty-three), 116-117
liminal space
    Harvest Moon and, 115
    new moon in Taurus and, 74
    Samhain and, 2-3
Litha (June 21), 81-85
    ritual to embrace the power of the
        sun, 83-85
loaf-mass, 97-98, 99-100
Loki, 19
Long Night Moon, 23-24
Lugh/Lughnasadh, 98
lunar scrying, 46

Mabon (September 21), 109-113, 115
    ritual to embrace the darkness,
        112-113
magic, creating power of in everyday,
    127-128
Maiouma, 67
Maiwein (May Wine), 70, 72
malachite, 33
māna, 81
Mani, 82
manifestation anointing oil, creating
    a, 94-95
March moon (week seventeen), 55-56
May moon (week twenty-five), 73-74
maypole, 69-72
May Queen, 67-69, 71
moonstone, 33, 95, 116

moon water, 78

Morrigan, 20-21

mulled wine, 21

new moon
  in Aquarius (week fourteen), 43-44
  in Aries (week twenty-two), 61-63
  in Cancer (week thirty-four), 91-92
  in Capricorn (week ten), 29-30
  of Gemini (week thirty), 87
  in Leo (week thirty-eight), 103-104
  in Libra (week forty-six), 121-122
  in Pisces (week eighteen), 56-57
  in Sagittarius (week six), 24-25
  in Scorpio (week two), 10-11
  in Taurus (week twenty-six), 74-75
  in Virgo (week forty-two), 115-116

night of the walking dead, 2-6

November moon, light of the (week one), 9-10

Oak King, 21, 81, 109

obsidian, 11, 27, 91

October moon (week forty-five), 120-121

Odin, 19

ofrendas, 5-6

Olwen, 110

onyx, 11

opal, 8, 31

Ophelia, 20

Ostara (March 21), 49-54, 68, 111
  ritual to find balance, 51-54
  spring salad, 54

Pan, 19-20, 67

pentagram, 106

Persephone, 68, 110

pine, 19-20, 21

Pink Moon, 60-61

Pisces
  full moon in (week forty-four), 118-119
  new moon in (week eighteen), 56-57

sun in (week fifteen), 44-45

Pitys, 19-20

pyrite, 95

reaper, Samhain and, 3 7

red jasper, 31

regrets, Samhain and, 4, 7

rhodochrosite, 33

ribbons
  maypole, 69, 71-72
  May Queen and, 68

rose quartz, 33, 74, 117, 123

rowan, 8

Ruadán, 36

ruby, 11

Sagittarius
  full moon in (week thirty-two),
    89-90
  new moon in (week six), 24-25
  sun in (week three), 12-13
  St. Brigid's Day, 35-40

salad, spring, 54

Samasthiti, 83

Samhain (October 31), 1-15
  night of the walking dead, 2-6
  ritual to connect with your walking
    dead, 6-8

Scorpio
  full moon in (week twenty-eight),
    77-78
  new moon in (week two), 10-11
  sun in (week forty-seven), 122-123

Season of the Witch, 1

selenite, 27, 117

self-care, 88-89

September moon (week forty-one),
  114-115

sheela na gig, 35-36

sigil, creating a, 93

singing, Yule ritual and, 22

smoky quartz, 27, 91

Snow Moon, 41–42

Sol, 82

spell bag, 13

spell jar
    Litha and, 84–85
    sun in Aquarius and, 31

spring cleaning, 52–53

spring equinox. *See* Ostara (March 21)

Storm Moon, 41–42

Strawberry Moon, 86

Sturgeon Moon, 102–103

sugilite, 31

summer solstice. *See* Litha (June 21)

sun
    in Aquarius (week eleven), 30–32
    in Aries (week nineteen), 57–58
    in Cancer (week thirty-one), 88–89
    in Capricorn (week seven), 25–26
    in Gemini (week twenty-seven),
        75–77
    in Leo (week thirty-five), 92–93
    in Libra (week forty-three), 116–117
    in Pisces (week fifteen), 44–45
    ritual to embrace the power of the,
        83–85
    in Sagittarius (week three), 12–13
    in Scorpio (week forty-seven),
        122–123
    in Taurus (week twenty-three),
        63–64
    in Virgo (week thirty-nine), 104–105

sun gods, 81–82, 98

Susanoo, 81–82

Tailtiu, 98, 100–101

talisman, 13

task-mastering spell, 26

Taurus
    full moon in (week four), 14–15
    new moon in (week twenty-six),
        74–75
    sun in (week twenty-three), 63–64

third eye chakra *(ajna)*
    anointing, 30, 70–71, 78, 121
    connecting with, 57

Thunder Moon, 91–92

tigereye, 13, 31, 92

Toll, Maia, 82

tourmaline, 11

truth serum, crafting, 120–121

Tuatha dé Danann, 36

turquoise, 13

Twrch Trwyth, 110

Virgo
    full moon in (week twenty), 59–60
    new moon in (week forty-two),
        115–116
    sun in (week thirty-nine), 104–105

wassailing, 22

wells, Brigid and, 37–38

wildness within, ritual to explore,
    69–72

Wild Wisdom Companion (Toll), 82

willow, 8

winter solstice. *See* Yule (December 21)

Wolf Moon, 28–29

Worm Moon, 55–56

wreaths, 21–22

yew, 20–21

Ysbaddaden Bencawr, 110

Yule (December 21), 17–22
    Holly King, 18–21
    ritual to find light in the darkness,
        21–22

Yule altar, 22

yule log, 22

zombies, 2